THE FAITHFUL SCIENTIST

The Faithful Scientist

Experiences of Anti-Religious Bias in Scientific Training

Christopher P. Scheitle

NEW YORK UNIVERSITY PRESS

New York

NEW YORK UNIVERSITY PRESS
New York
www.nyupress.org

Please contact the Library of Congress for Cataloging-in-Publication data.
ISBN: 9781479823710 (hardback)
ISBN: 9781479823765 (library ebook)
ISBN: 9781479823741 (consumer ebook)

This book is printed on acid-free paper, and its binding materials are chosen for strength and durability. We strive to use environmentally responsible suppliers and materials to the greatest extent possible in publishing our books.

Manufactured in the United States of America

10 9 8 7 6 5 4 3 2 1

Also available as an ebook

For Lisa, Avery, and Sloane

CONTENTS

Introduction

Identity and Community

Danielle

Danielle was about half-way through her PhD program in physics. Like many graduate students, Danielle felt like an imposter for the first couple of years, but she was now starting to feel more confident as a physicist.

> I don't know what it was, but basically when I started getting it, when it started clicking, and I realized I can actually do this hard stuff. I got past the basic classes, and I was like, "Actually, I'm understanding physics," and I could talk to physicists at the same level or I'm getting there. It was basically, I think, maybe the beginning of my third year when I was finishing up quantum mechanics, and for the first time, and I was just like, "I get quantum mechanics. Oh my gosh." When that happened, that was kind of a milestone for me . . . and I was reaffirmed by other friends of mine who were further ahead in the program and they were like, "I think you'll be just fine." Hearing that from them, and also seeing that I could do it, was very reaffirming for me, and that's when I felt like, "I'm a physicist."[1]

As a Black woman, Danielle's experience was understandably shaped by the extreme underrepresentation of others within physics sharing her race, gender, and the intersection between the two.[2] She pointed to the mentoring she received from other women in physics as having a powerful effect on her trajectory. Danielle said of her undergraduate physics mentor, "I feel like if she had not been my professor, I don't know if I would have continued on." In talking about some of the challenges she had faced in grad school, she shared that "sometimes I feel threatened being in a room full of White people . . . like, unwelcome in some way," she told me. "No one said welcome, but no one said you're not welcome. It was just kind of like, you know, so I just [hid] in the back." She also shared with me several instances of Black students she knew on campus being treated in ways that seemed to have been motivated by bias. Despite the many challenges, being part of multiple minority groups in science had also presented Danielle with a sense of purpose. "I feel like I'm rebranding physicists in my own way. A physicist doesn't necessarily have to be a White man in a plaid shirt," she said.

Although her race and gender were obviously essential components of her life and identity, Danielle pointed to another component as having the primary salience for her sense of identity and community. "For some people, [science] is the end-all be-all. That defines them. 'I am a physicist,' point blank. But for me, that's not who I am. I'm a Christian. I'm a child of God, number one, and then I'm a physicist." Indeed, Danielle told me that she had always been very involved in practices connected to her faith.

> I go to church. I pray. I worship God. . . . Worship is a lifestyle. It's how you live your life. I sing to God, and I play guitar. Things like that. I went to Israel. That was cool. I did campus ministry. It was my job to be a Christian and to help people to discover faith.

Danielle's faith had played a significant role in shaping her path within science. Before committing to physics, she had thought she might pursue a medical degree.

> How I actually came to want to study physics was I prayed. I prayed about surrendering my dream of being a doctor to God. I just said, "God, I hold my hands open to you if you want me to be a doctor then open those doors. If not, open some other door." Then a series of events happened where I ended up doing this other thing, and that was a huge shift for me, at least in my life events and my life goals.

Being a Christian had brought its own challenges in terms of feeling welcome within the scientific community. Danielle described to me various types of "offhanded comments" that she heard other students and faculty make about religion. "One guy making fun saying, 'This is not a church.' You could sense the not-niceness and his maybe spite coming toward people who are believers." Danielle also recounted how she once saw Neil deGrasse Tyson—the well-known physicist and science communicator—give a talk at a conference. "I just remembered being a Christian, and he was saying some not-nice comments about Christians. I remembered feeling uncomfortable in that setting."

Danielle also struggled with more subtle tensions resulting from her religious identity. For instance, throughout our conversation, she interweaved talking about her faith with talking about her family—both the family she grew up with and the family she wanted to create in the future. She told me that her time as an undergraduate was spiritually challenging "because [she] was away from my mom who raised me to have a faith in God." She also described to me how it was difficult to be unable to visit her family as much as she wanted given the demands of her graduate program. She saw her emerging scientific career as a potential obstacle to starting her own family.

I value family and ultimately that's something I want. I've heard horror stories and actually seen some things where people [in science] were discouraged from having children. [People say,] "Oh, that's going take away from your productivity." And that was something that I didn't like to see. That's something I want, so if that's not important here, then I'll just do something else or go someplace else where it is normal. Because it is normal.

Given such messages, Danielle had at times worried about how her religious identity, the values that resulted from that identity, and her involvement in a religious community would be perceived by others in her physics program or within the scientific community in general. Although she could point to a couple of students and possibly one or two faculty members in her program she knew were religious, she told me that "most people that I've met are not religious" or are even hostile to religion ("Anti or whatever," as she put it). She said that being Christian "used to get in the way a lot. I would tiptoe around that, because I serve at church and a lot of times I'm leaving to go to do something to serve in some way. And so I used to feel like I'd be ridiculed for that. But now I just don't care anymore."

Despite some of the messages she had received that seem hostile to religion, Danielle did not see any tension between her faith and her scientific interests.

> I don't dissociate the two whatsoever. I see them as one and the same because I see God made the universe, I study the universe, so I'm studying God's handiwork. I feel like the stars are declaring God's praise. I'm declaring God's praise. It's kind of one and the same, and I think it's a beautiful, harmonious thing. I feel like my whole life is worshiping God or is about God's praise.

Danielle's experience as a religious individual training to be a scientist raises a number of interesting and important questions—questions that are often lost in discussions about religion and science, which often tend to focus on either abstract philosophical principles or hot-button political and moral debates. Do religious scientists struggle with internal theological tensions between their faith and their scientific pursuits, as so much of the larger conversation about religion and science would lead us to assume? Or might the tensions experienced by religious scientists be more social and external in nature? How might religious scientists view their life and career differently from nonreligious scientists? And what is or should be the role of religion in the larger effort to support diversity in science? How might religion affect the ability of science to recruit women and racial minorities into science, and should religion itself be seen as an important dimension of diversity to consider within science? These are some of the questions the following chapters will explore using survey and interview data from graduate students pursuing PhDs in five natural and social science disciplines.

To begin, it is important to consider how we think about religion, science, and the relationship between the two. While religion and science both make claims about the physical world and make explicit or implicit value claims, we must recognize that their shared and sometimes conflicting functions go beyond these two domains. Both religion and science also represent social institutions consisting of individuals who identify with them and communities that support and reproduce those identities.

Knowledge and Morals

It is tempting to see religion and science as sharing little in common. Indeed, much discussion and writing on religion and science highlights the differences between the two. We are told, for instance, that "in contrast to science . . . religion adjudicates truth not empirically, but via dogma, scripture and authority."[3]

But, like siblings whose frequent tiffs mask the fact that their tensions arise from being so much alike, religion and science actually do share much in common. As the previous quotation suggests, both religion and science make claims about the physical world. While such claims are at the heart of science, the nature and importance of such claims vary across and within religious communities. Nonetheless, the shared function of making truth claims about the physical world is often pointed to as the reason why religion and science are in conflict with each other.[4] There are a couple of problems with this conclusion.

First, analyses of survey data by social scientists have found the evidence of conflict over such truth claims to be pretty limited. Yes, if you ask people whether they accept scientific claims that have strong connections to theological claims—such as regarding evolution—individuals who are more religious tend to be more likely to "reject" them. Such "religiously contested" scientific facts, though, are limited and often have little to do with the day-to-day work of science. As the sociologist John Evans has noted, "religious people have not been opposed to scientific claims of how photosynthesis works because these claims do not contradict any religious claims."[5] Indeed, studies have found that if you ask about scientific claims without such obvious religious connotations, religious individuals are just as likely to accept the scientific consensus as anyone else.[6] And even for those theologically charged topics like evolution, research has found that most religious people are actually quite flexible in what creation-evolution narrative they will accept as long as they see some potential role for God within that narrative.[7]

The other problem with the hyper-focus on the knowledge claims of religion and science is that it ignores the other aspects or functions shared by both religion and science and the tensions that can result from these other forms of overlap. For instance, religion and science are both driven by explicit and implicit value systems, which can lead to moral conflicts between the two. Such moral value claims are most obvious in the case of religion, but science is also frequently guided by implicit values. Medical science, for instance, is often guided by the core values of reducing suffering and extending life by any means possible. In cases like embryonic stem cell research, this value might run counter to other values taught by religion.[8] In such cases, conflict—*moral* conflict, not conflict over knowledge—results between religion and science.

Identity and Community

But religion and science represent more than just written lists of (occasionally) competing truth claims and moral values. They are also social institutions. That is, they each consist of individuals and communities who hold and continually reproduce social identities through shared norms and social interactions. Social identity is multifaceted. Most concretely, it provides a sense of membership to some group. But that identity—and the group it is connected to—also provides a framework for understanding our own purpose and provides guidance for how to pursue that purpose. Our social identity is thus often our source of meaning. An individual's social identity can be derived from a variety of sources, such as family, work, nationality, and so on.[9] It is fairly intuitive to see religion as a source of identity. We are accustomed to hearing people explicitly identifying with their religion ("I am Muslim."). And we often see people connecting their faith to a sense of meaning or a course of action in their lives.

Although it is less obvious to see science as a social identity, it is not entirely difficult to understand either. It might be easiest to think of science as a social identity when thinking specifically about scientists. It is common for an individual's work to be a significant source of social identity. After all, one of the first questions we often ask of someone we meet is "what do you do?"—signaling the assumed importance of work to one's sense of self. The identity-work connection might be particularly strong for occupations—or professions—requiring advanced levels of education and training.[10] That training and education often instills a feeling of membership into a unique group that the individual belongs to and provides them with a sense of purpose in their lives. An individual expressing that they are "a scientist," then, is rarely making a simple statement about what they do for a paycheck. Rather, it is a statement of belonging, pride, meaning, and values.[11]

The identity-laden nature of "science" can be seen among non-scientists, too, especially with the increasing politicization of science.[12] Yard signs and bumper stickers expressing support for science are rarely just a simple expression of, say, advocacy for increased funding for scientific research. Instead, they often implicitly or explicitly express the individual's identification with a broader value system and social group.[13]

Religion and science are also both sources of community and belonging. They both influence the people we spend time with, the places we go, the groups and organizations we belong to, and even sometimes where we live and work. Religion often leads individuals to attend a particular congregation or participate in religious activities that shape their social connections. Similarly, scientific training and professional organizations provide opportunities for individuals to connect with others in their field, leading to a sense of belonging within the scientific community. These connections can become an individual's primary source of social support. This may be most apparent when considering the ways scientists interact. Scientists and individuals pursuing a career in science often attend the same universities and conferences, where they work and learn together. These shared experiences can lead to the formation of strong friendships and other types of relationships that can dominate the social networks of scientists. Even among individuals who may not be employed as scientists, an interest or passion for science can shape their social circles. For example, they may choose to visit science museums instead of attending sporting events, or enroll their children in science-themed summer camps. These choices can lead to connections with other scientifically-minded individuals and organizations.

It is not surprising that an individual's social identity and community are closely intertwined. An individual's identity can drive the behaviors and associations that form and solidify a community. In other cases, a person's community precedes a strong sense of identity. That is, chance encounters may lead to new friendships or activities, which then lay the groundwork for the individual to identify with a particular social group.[14] Regardless of which comes first, once established, social identity and community tend to reinforce each other.

Individuals typically have multiple social identities and associated communities. A person might strongly identify as a father, as a physician, and as a Dallas Cowboys fan, for example. These identities can shape the individual's social activities and associations. Sometimes identities and communities can compete with each other, such as when one identity is particularly demanding and leaves little time or energy for others. For instance, a medical doctor working in a demanding environment like an emergency room might have little room for serious identification or association with anything outside of work.[15]

In other cases, conflict between two social identities can result from one community looking negatively upon another identity or viewing identification with that community as incompatible with their own. For example, it might be difficult to simultaneously be a committed Dallas Cowboys fan and a committed Philadelphia Eagles fan because it would be seen as counter-stereotypical (i.e., unusual). Even if one did hold both identities, it would be difficult to seamlessly move between the activities and social groups associated with each fan base. An individual would likely need to conceal their identity with one group from the other and vice versa.

Having one foot in the religious community and another in the scientific community is generally seen as counter-stereotypical. In short, many people see being a religious scientist as strange. Why is holding a religious identity seen as incompatible with holding a scientist identity, and vice versa? Historians have often tried to convince the public and other scholars that religion and science have not always been seen as incompatible and that being a religious scientist was not always seen as odd.[16]

The sociologist Thomas Gieryn has argued that the emergence of a strong boundary between the identities and communities of religion and science can be traced to scientists' efforts to garner more attention, prestige, and resources within society. To make their case, prominent scientists and scientific organizations began to draw stronger lines between what science and scientists do in comparison to religion as well as to, interestingly, more applied fields like engineering and manufacturing. This boundary-drawing effort began in earnest in the nineteenth century, but Gieryn argues that it is constantly being repeated, up to and including today. To be clear, these scientists were not only making the case that they and their efforts were *different* from religion and those applied fields, but also *superior* to them. As Gieryn suggests, the credibility of science and the scientific community became dependent on maintaining a boundary between science and those other institutions. This boundary work created a social rift, making it more difficult to identify with and be a part of both the religious and scientific communities. Think of those disaster movies where a suddenly appearing chasm in the ground isolates two individuals or groups from each other.[17] From this perspective, the presence of *religious scientists* would seem to threaten the clarity of that boundary, as they are trying to reach across it.[18]

Due to their counter-stereotypical nature, religious scientists face challenges as they try to bridge the gap between their identities and communities. When we talk about conflict between religion and science, especially religion-science conflict *as experienced by individuals trying to navigate both social worlds*, these types of identity-based and community-based conflicts have often been overlooked in favor of focusing on apparent theological-epistemological conflicts (e.g., science says this about the physical world, but religion says this) or moral conflicts (e.g., scientists want to do this or teach this, but religious communities are opposed).

Being Counter-Stereotypical

In the mid-twentieth century, the eminent sociologist Robert Merton wrote that the culture of science represents an

> affectively toned complex of values and norms which is held to be binding on the man of science. The norms are expressed in the form of prescription, proscriptions and permissions. These are legitimatized in terms of institutional values. These imperatives, transmitted by precept and example and reenforced by sanctions, are in varying degrees internalized by the scientist, thus fashioning his 'scientific conscience' or, if one prefers the latter-day phrase, his superego.[19]

In other words, individuals who enter the culture of science adopt the values and identity of that culture and are subject to the rules and sanctions of that scientific community. As Merton notes, these rules and sanctions are often internalized within the scientist, meaning that formal rules and sanctions are rarely needed and remain unspoken. Scientists largely adopt the identity and community of their profession, while avoiding other identities and communities that may be seen as threatening to their status as scientists. This prevents individuals from experiencing the social and psychological costs of being seen as counter-stereotypical.

Yet sometimes the unspoken rules of an identity and its community are verbalized. In my conversations with people about religion and science over the years, I have found that people will often comment on whether a person can be both a scientist and religious at the same time. Someone might say, "I don't think it's unreasonable to be both religious or spiritual and a scientist."[20] Or "you can totally be a scientist and be religious."[21] Or, when talking about someone else, some might say "he's religious, but I still say he's a great scientist."[22]

While on the surface, such statements may seem to be arguing against the counter-stereotypical status of being a religious scientist, there seems to be more uncertainty below this surface. Indeed, it is noteworthy that I never actually asked an interview subject whether it is possible to be both religious and a scientist. It would be a poor question to ask because there are many examples of highly accomplished scientists who are also serious about their faith. As a yes–no question, it seems like a question that does not need to be asked.

In fact, many of the people who have told me that they think an individual can be both a scientist and religious *are religious scientists themselves and are therefore evidence of the answer to that question.* Yet there still seems to be an urge to state this explicitly in conversation. My sense from these conversations is that individuals are aware that being religious and being a scientist is largely seen as going against the culture of science, so they are trying to preemptively counter any sense of dissonance they may feel within our conversation or discordance they assume I perceive them to represent.

Robert Merton, writing elsewhere, argued that the apparent tension between the culture of science and other cultures is often "non-logical" and tied simply to a "feeling of incompatibility between the sentiments embodied in the scientific ethos" and the culture outside of science.[23]

That is, there is a *feeling* that identifying as religious means you cannot or should not identify as a scientist, and a *sense* that scientists do not really associate with religious people. Religion and science are seen as representing different teams, and it would be counter-stereotypical for someone to be a member of both.[24]

From this perspective, there is nothing inherent that prevents someone from being a religious scientist. However, there are strong social-psychological barriers to being a religious scientist. Religious individuals do enter science and, as a result, they must navigate those social and psychological tensions. While it might be interesting to explore these tensions among established scientists,[25] it is even more revealing to examine these tensions among emerging or nascent scientists. Unlike established members of a culture or community, neophytes are more likely to intentionally or unintentionally reveal the hidden and unspoken values and norms of that culture because they are actively probing and learning those norms themselves. But what does it mean to be a nascent or emerging scientist?

Becoming a Scientist

When does someone become a scientist? There are different ways to answer this question. Is it when they start to think of themselves as a scientist? Is it when they obtain employment as a scientist? Although we can point to different indicators, most of those would lead us back to a similar point in time: graduate school, especially obtaining a doctorate in a scientific field.

Young children and teens can certainly have some level of identification with science and see themselves as scientists one day. College students can obtain their bachelor's degrees in science, and such degrees might land a person in a science-related occupation. However, the jobs typically associated with being a "scientist" and having an associated title—"biologist," "chemist," and so on—tend to require a graduate degree.

Graduate programs in science, especially PhD programs, are generally where individuals obtain the credentials needed to obtain employment as a formal scientist. More importantly, though, it is in these programs where individuals *gain an identity as a scientist and start to join the social organization of science.* To the extent that adopting that identity and joining that social organization is in tension with having a religious identity and being a part of a religious social organization, it is in graduate science programs where we can best understand how religious scientists navigate and respond to this tension.

The Graduate School Setting

Some have described PhD programs as akin to taking children and turning them into adults. Individuals start graduate school as "infants" with "limited professional awareness, skills, and understanding, and an undeveloped sense of professional identity."[26] Graduate programs reshape these lumps of clay not only into individuals with particular knowledge and skills, but also into individuals who embrace a particular identity and its accompanying social organization. That is, science PhD programs create scientists who become part of the scientific community.

Science PhD programs, of course, are not the only or even the most extreme example of individuals being reshaped into new identities and communities. When thinking of such processes, many might first think of how the military takes new recruits and turns them into soldiers. This not only involves training soldiers in technical skills and knowledge but also instilling in them the identity of a soldier and a sense of loyalty to the military community.[27]

Interestingly, we might think of graduate school as similar to the process of being socialized into a new religious group. Some have explicitly compared being a part of a PhD program to such a religious socialization experience. In giving advice to future and current PhD students, Matt Might, a professor of medicine and computer science, argued that students should come to see their PhD program as "neither school nor work. [It] is a monastic experience. [It] demands contemplative labor on days, nights, and weekends. [It] takes biblical levels of devotion. [It] even comes with built-in vows of poverty and obedience. The end brings an ecclesiastical robe and a clerical hood."[28]

To those unfamiliar with how PhD programs work, these comparisons may seem strange. Indeed, while a significant portion of the public has some sense of what it is like to be an undergraduate college student—either through personal experience, through the experiences of friends and family, or through portrayals in the media—only a tiny slice of the public will pursue a doctoral degree or even have much exposure to the experience of a PhD student.[29] While it might be tempting to think of such PhD programs as simply "more college," this misses the substantial social, pedagogical, and cultural differences between undergraduate and graduate programs.

To be clear, many graduate students do not fully appreciate these unique dynamics themselves when they enter their PhD programs, and may be thinking that they are just doing "more college." As sociologist Jessica Calarco has noted, students are often left on their own to figure out the "hidden curriculum" of grad school, and those who do not make these adjustments usually do not succeed.[30] This hidden curriculum not only consists of figuring out the bureaucratic procedures and structure of PhD programs—What is "comps"? What does it mean to be "ABD"?—but also the more subtle social and cultural mores of PhD programs and the larger scientific community.

A PhD program typically takes a minimum of five years to complete after obtaining a bachelor's degree, although many students take closer to seven or more years to finish.[31] This is a significant portion of one's life, occurring when many similarly aged peers are advancing in their careers and starting their families. This only feeds into the monastic feeling of graduate school as students forsake worldly pursuits for knowledge and credentials acquired by a proud few. As PhD students' life courses diverge from their peers outside of graduate school, their PhD program and scientific pursuits become the center of their social world and, in turn, their identities.

While undergraduates might often feel nameless, shifting across a large campus between classes with thousands of other students, PhD programs tend to represent small social bubbles within the much larger university environment. Each year a PhD program may only accept a handful of students, and the entire program may consist of only a few dozen students. Students will tend to spend most of their time in a single building where their offices, classes, and laboratories are located.

PhD students are often paid—albeit minimally— to teach and assist with faculty research and are usually formally or informally prevented from seeking out other work. Students usually work under the mentorship of a single faculty member who has significant influence on the student's experience in graduate school and their career after graduate school. While PhD students will take some classes, especially in their first two years of the program, most of their time and effort is dedicated to working on research and developing their curriculum vitae, which, if the stakes were not clear enough, is Latin for "course of life." A meager curriculum vitae then becomes evidence of a meager life for scientists.

Given the intense, immersive, and long-term nature of obtaining a PhD in science, it would be difficult for the experience not to result in significant changes to one's identity and community. Indeed, if a student obtained a PhD in science but did not think of themselves as a scientist or as part of the scientific community, it would represent a significant failure of the program.

But what if a graduate student holds another identity and is part of another community that is seen by others as antithetical to being a scientist or being in the scientific community? How does such a student experience those perceptions and assumptions? Or what if the values and priorities emphasized by that other identity and community are in tension with the values and priorities emphasized by the scientist identity and community? How does a student balance those competing messages? These are some of the core questions that the following chapters will consider.

The importance and implications of such questions are not purely intellectual. Calls for increasing the size and diversity of the scientific workforce appear with regularity.[32] Religious individuals represent a sizable share of the US population, making them an important part of the overall strategy for increasing the scientific workforce. Moreover, religious diversity is often strongly associated with other forms of diversity, such as racial and ethnic diversity. Identity- or community-driven barriers to thriving in science that are connected to religion could have important implications for science's efforts to incorporate more people of color. If diversity in science is beneficial because it brings new ideas and different perspectives to scientific workplaces, education, and outreach, then religious diversity itself would seem to be a natural contributor to that dynamic.

The Study

Over the past few years, I have surveyed over 1,300 graduate students pursuing PhDs in five natural and social science disciplines in the United States: physics, chemistry, biology, psychology, and sociology.[33] I have also conducted in-depth interviews with over fifty of these students, with a particular focus on interviewing students who describe themselves as religious. (For those interested, more information about my research methods and data can be found in the appendices.)

These quantitative and qualitative data provide unique insights into how these nascent religious scientists experience conflict between religion and science—not because of any epistemological or theological reasons—but because of tensions between the identities and associated communities tied to their religious faith and their emerging scientific careers.

Though it is not the first to examine issues of religion among scientists, this book is unique in its focus on graduate students, who, given their liminal state, are a particularly interesting group to consider when thinking about questions of identity and community.[34] The first two chapters examine the religious lives of science graduate students and their perspectives on theological and scientific questions about the relationship between religion and science. The remaining chapters move beyond these issues to look more deeply at how the identities and communities of science and religion create tensions for nascent scientists, particularly those who are religious themselves.

1

The Religious Lives of Scientists-in-Training

Mark and Adhira

Mark was a chemistry student approaching the end of his PhD program. He came from an academic family, with his father being a professor and his mom a high school teacher. This background may explain his early interest in becoming a teacher himself, specifically a science teacher. He remembered wanting to work for NASA when he was six years old, a dream that remained with him for many years. "In high school I really didn't like physics, and I really liked chemistry, so I decided I would just go ahead and try that." As an undergraduate, Mark was a chemistry and French major and found himself at one point "very passionate about French." However, as he became more involved with research in the chemistry department, he decided to pursue a PhD in that area.[1]

Although he described his overall experience in graduate school as "very positive," there had been bumps in the road, including an abrupt change in his advisor and research focus.

> I definitely had some challenging times, things that make grad school not very fun. Things that make you kind of question whether you want to continue or leave . . . not in my program specifically, but just PhD programs in general. It was something where my wife certainly had a very eye-opening experience being married to a grad student. She would basically never recommend a PhD to anyone, unless they really, really needed it for something.

Mark noted that a significant reason he was able to overcome some of the obstacles thrown at him during his PhD program was the support he derived from people outside of his school life. "It's been something where having a community, having people that I know and trust, even though they don't really understand what I'm going through, I get to see that kind of outside world and realize grad school is not the entirety of life. For me, that was through my church."

That he looked to a religious community for support during his science PhD program is not particularly surprising, considering Mark's religious upbringing.

> I grew up in a Christian household. My mom in particular is a very strong Christian. I was also homeschooled, so she had some say in our curriculum. She was very active in our spiritual faith, in getting into the Bible, and studying the Bible, and kind of how even before I was a Christian, like oh this is what Christians think, and this is how people should structure society, that sort of thing.

As an undergraduate, Mark went through a period of questioning some of his previous beliefs and perceptions.

> That was one of the first times that I can remember, I was extremely divided on what I believed in, and had to then start deciding okay, I'm still a Christian, but what does that mean for me? It was great. I think that's honestly how those things are supposed to be, because then it was, "okay I need to then get back into reading the Bible, and thinking about this thing here, my life, am I doing this just because my family says this is how we do it, or is this because this is actually the right or wrong way to do it?"

Mark began to attend a Presbyterian church during graduate school. "I started in a Baptist church with my family, went to this non-denominational church in college, and I'm now at a Presbyterian church." When he met his wife, who came from a Lutheran background,

Mark had to revisit his own beliefs and identity again. "We might disagree, or have different beliefs, but our core beliefs [are the same], like our beliefs toward what is salvation [and] our beliefs toward the scriptures themselves." Mark concluded his description of his religious trajectory by stating, "My faith is extremely fundamental to my identity, to who I am, the way that I perceive things."

Adhira was starting her fourth year in a PhD program in biology. She came to the United States from India for her undergraduate degree. A fortuitous connection with a mentor got her involved in research as an undergrad and subsequently motivated her to pursue graduate school. She was the first in her family to attend college in any form and feels pressure to succeed "for my family and my [undergraduate] mentor."[2]

Graduate school had been challenging at times for Adhira, as it is for many students.

> It's the isolation and imposter syndrome. Isolation in the sense that undergrads are very well-rounded persons doing a lot of different things, [but] in grad school you're required to fully focus on lab stuff and not do other things. Also, being an extrovert, I never realized that science or lab stuff attracts introverts, and it's hard connecting to my lab mates. I just realized that they just don't want to connect. And then the whole imposter syndrome. . . . It was a big deal getting into a PhD program for me, but when I came here it was almost like, "oh, everyone gets a PhD, it's not that big of a deal." It was hard to see where I fit in, and instead of having that support so I could figure out where I fit in, you came in and then you just started working the next day. I feel like it's hard to do only one thing, and you don't have anything else balancing it out.

Adhira described herself as a "spiritual Hindu," which she distinguished from her father, whom she described as "religious." As we talk more, I sense that this religious-versus-spiritual distinction for Adhira hinged on believing in various sorts of supernatural interventions more than particular religious practices or even general religious beliefs like a belief in a God. She told me at one point, "I wouldn't think I'm failing in grad school because God isn't happy with me or something like that, or like God's going to save my experiment."

She said her upbringing was very open in terms of her own beliefs and practices. "My dad never forced me to pray to the same god that he does . . . we were never forced to fast or anything. [My parents] never forced us to follow them or do anything."

When I asked Adhira about the relationship between religion and science, and the perception that some might have of conflict, she simply said, "I don't think there is a conflict. . . . They're two different parts of my identity. I don't think they blend into each other. They bring out different fulfillment for me." While Adhira did not see conflict between religion and science—at least in some grand theological or moral sense—as we talked more, it became clear that there had been some more practical tensions between religion and science within her own life.

While her religion might have served as the source of balance that Adhira said she desired, there had been obstacles to achieving this balance. Going to grad school had led to changes in her life that had affected her sense of identity and community, which had disconnected her from her faith.

> It's hard . . . I came here in 2011. So a big part of my identity is shaped being here. If we're being honest, there are no temples here or anything. I have statues in my house. Maybe if there was a temple, maybe I would go there. But there are not that many resources for me to embrace my spiritual identity in a way.

Adhira pointed to the demanding life of grad school as a key reason for her reduced spiritual practice.

> I used to fast. And I stopped doing that since I've gone to grad school, because it's really, really hard to fast when you're doing work. Fasting is

not eating or drinking anything the whole day. And you're expected to do work, it's not like you can . . . well, I don't know. I've never thought about asking to take the day off to practice it. So I wouldn't know if I would be able to do that.

She also told me that her spirituality played a role in her passion for volunteering, but this practice had been curtailed as well in grad school.

Volunteering is a big part of who I am. I had this meeting with my boss to talk about what my long-term goals are, and she's like, "You're expected to do lab work." And I was like, "I'm doing it." But she was like, "I don't want you doing anything else but lab." And I was like, "You really don't understand that this is one of my core values." So, I don't think our core values match.

Still, Adhira made some effort to express her faith when possible, and hoped to revisit other parts of her spirituality in the future.

When our main festival comes—which is Diwali—I go buy some sweets and I get them for my lab mates. And whether they choose to eat it, it's their decision. But this is me expressing my religious identity. I'm hoping that starting this year, I can do the fasting again. Seeing my lab mate do the Ramadan thing, I think it really empowered me. That fast, I've done since I was fourteen. It's important to me, and the fact that I haven't done it for the past three years, it's kind of sad.

In many contexts in the United States, Mark and Adhira's religiosity would be quite ordinary. While there has been much interest in the growing proportion of the population who do not identify with a religion,[3] a large portion of the American population is still quite religious. Over 50 percent of American adults say that they have no doubts about the existence of God, and about 50 percent also report praying once a day or more. Other surveys find that Americans identify religion as one of the most important sources of meaning in their lives, second only to their family.[4] The Pew Research Center's analysis, examining a wide variety of religious beliefs and behaviors, classifies about four in ten Americans as "highly religious," with another three in ten classified as "somewhat religious."[5]

Despite being relatively mundane in larger American society, Mark and Adhira's religiosity would strike many as curious, given their pursuit of a doctorate and career in science. The idea that scientists are usually not religious, if not outright hostile toward religion, is prominent in our culture. Television, film, and literature often present religious people and scientists in opposing roles, such as Jodie Foster's atheist scientist in the movie *Contact* being juxtaposed with Matthew McConaughey's theologian.[6] Or consider the television show *The Big Bang Theory*, which juxtaposes its central character, Sheldon, a brilliant and religiously skeptical physicist, with his religious and scientifically skeptical mother.[7] Beyond such popular culture images, though, what do we know about the religiosity of scientists?

Religiosity of Scientists: A Persistent Interest

Social scientists and the general public have consistently maintained an interest in the religious affiliations, practices, and beliefs of scientists. For social scientists, this interest has largely been driven by a larger interest in secularization—the hypothesis that religion would fade away as individuals and societies become more modernized. The exact meaning of "modernized" is often a bit fuzzy, but science has typically been a major component of this modernization and secularization process.[8] As individuals become more knowledgeable about science, the argument goes, religion will no longer be needed because it mainly serves the purpose of providing a mechanism for understanding how the world works. Science not only provides an alternative framework for that understanding, but one that often undercuts the plausibility of religious belief.

In the larger context of this process, scientists serve as a type of canary in the coal mine. Since they are highly exposed to the methods and findings of science, they should represent the leading edge of secularization. In short, scientists should be the first to give up, if not forcibly reject, religious affiliation, belief, and practice.

The psychologist James Leuba was the first to try to systematically measure the religiosity of scientists.[9] In 1916, he sent a survey to scientists listed in a volume called *American Men of Science*, as well as to membership lists of various professional organizations. The survey asked about the scientists' belief in God and their belief in immortality (i.e., an afterlife). The responses showed that only about 44% of physical scientists and 31% of biological scientists stated a belief in God, while only about 51% of physical scientists and 37% of biological scientists expressed a belief in immortality. Leuba does not provide a comparison to non-scientists, but these percentages would have likely approached 100% among the general public in 1916.[10]

Although the rate of belief among scientists was relatively low, Leuba expressed some surprise that the percentages were not lower and almost frustration that so many scientists expressed any belief at all. In discussing some scientists' belief in immortality, Leuba wrote, "The facts and the arguments known to my correspondents are apparently quite insufficient to convince all those who would find satisfaction in the expectation of an afterlife."[11]

Over the following hundred years, a number of social scientists have replicated Leuba's original study, including Leuba himself, in the 1930s.[12] In the 1990s, for instance, Larson and Witham published two studies presenting results from their replications. Their first study found that the *overall* rate of belief in God among scientists had held fairly steady between the 1910s and 1990s (42% to 39%).[13] On the other hand, in a follow-up study, Larson and Witham found that when looking only at more distinguished or "greater" scientists, the rate of belief in God had seemed to drop substantially from the 1910s.[14] These two studies were published with the somewhat confusing-when-juxtaposed titles of "Scientists are still keeping the faith" and "Leading scientists still reject God."

One of the limitations of Leuba's studies and those that have replicated them is their limited breadth and depth of measurement, at least by today's standards.[15] Leuba only asked about two issues: belief in God and belief in immortality/afterlife. Religiosity is, of course, much more multidimensional than what is captured by just these two issues. Furthermore, the questions Leuba asked regarding these issues were fairly restricted in their response options. For belief in God, for instance, scientists could only respond in one of three ways:

1. I believe in a God to whom one may pray in the expectation of receiving an answer. By "answer," I mean more than the subjective, psychological effect of prayer.
2. I do not believe in a God as defined above.
3. I have no definite belief regarding this question.

Those answering 1 were labeled "believers," those answering 2 were labeled "disbelievers," and those answering 3 were labeled "agnostics and doubters."[16] Clearly, these categories are wanting in their lack of detail.

This is where Elaine Howard Ecklund's 2010 study comes into play.[17] Ecklund surveyed over 1,600 scientists across both natural and social science disciplines using a much more extensive set of questions about their views on religion, science, and the connections between the two. She also conducted nearly three hundred in-depth interviews with scientists who took her survey.

The statistics Ecklund gathered add some nuance to Leuba's findings. She found that 34% of scientists overall say that they do not believe in God at all, while only 9% state that they have no doubts about God's existence. In-between these poles, Ecklund found that 8% of scientists say they believe in a "higher power" that isn't God, another 5% report believing in God sometimes, and 14% say they "have some doubts" but do "believe in God."[18]

Although these categories provide some additional detail to Leuba's findings, you might still walk away from Ecklund's study with the bottom-line conclusion that scientists are quite irreligious when compared to Americans in general. This would be a valid conclusion, but there are several other equally valid conclusions that her research highlighted. First, there is a sizable minority of scientists who view their faith as an important part of their identity, not just outside of their laboratories but also within them. Just under 40% of the scientists she surveyed, for example, felt that their religious or spiritual beliefs influenced their interactions with students and colleagues.

Another important conclusion from Ecklund's research, pertinent to the focus of this book, is that these religious scientists often struggle in balancing religion and science, but not because of the usual suspect issues like evolution and creation. Rather, they struggle with the social and cultural dimensions, as they feel that their scientist colleagues do not or would not tolerate their religious identity. These are issues I will explore further, in the context of graduate students in the sciences, but first let us review what we already know about the religiosity of scientists-in-training.

Religiosity of Scientists-in-Training

While the religiosity of scientists with established careers has been well explored, the religiosity of science students has received little attention. Some of this may be due to an assumption that studies of science professors already tell us what we need to know, as they were at one point science students themselves. There are reasons to think, though, that scientists-in-training may differ from their faculty teachers and mentors. Most obviously, there are often significant differences in age and generational cohorts between science students and their professors, which could lead to differences in religion and perceptions of the religion–science relationship.

More subtly, remember that most studies of scientists have focused on academic scientists, particularly those in more elite research universities. But not all science students will become science professors at research universities, whether due to issues of talent, life circumstances, or their career preferences. A survey of chemistry graduate students conducted by the American Chemical Society found that only 25 percent of doctoral students in chemistry say they are "very interested" in being a research-focused professor. More of these students report being "very interested" in being a teaching-focused professor (29%), researcher in industry (47%), or a researcher in a government agency (46%), not to mention students who expressed being interested in other paths.[19] If religion influences students' career interests, such as by leading to preferences outside of research-focused academic positions, then faculty at research-focused universities may not entirely mirror the religious composition of the graduate student population. In short, there are likely significant selection effects in who becomes a professor at a research university, as well as selection effects in who succeeds in completing their graduate program at all.

As previously mentioned, relatively few studies have examined the religiosity of scientists-in-training. The most comprehensive study on this issue is quite old. In 1963, sociologist Rodney Stark published results from a survey of graduate students. Stark found that "neophyte scientific scholars" were much less likely to be Protestant than the general public at the time (38% of students versus 66% of the public), while much more likely to be Jewish (9% versus 3%), some other religion (5% versus 1%), or religiously unaffiliated (26% versus 3%). The proportion of Catholic graduate students mirrored the population for the most part (22% versus 26%). In addition, Stark's survey showed that graduate students who scored higher on an index of "scholarly ethos" were less religious, and these students tended to be attending more prestigious graduate schools and had attended more prestigious schools as an undergraduate.

Based on his analysis of survey data, Stark argued that there are three general types of graduate students in terms of religion. The "uninvolved" student, who is typically found at more prestigious universities, may have been raised Protestant or Jewish but no longer identifies with any religion. This student links a significant part of their identity to their future profession and aims to gain a reputation as a prominent scholar. The "lowly involved" graduate student tends to be at a middle-tier university and only somewhat sees their graduate work as important to their sense of self. This student may continue to claim a religious affiliation, but does not attend religious services frequently. Finally, the "highly involved" graduate student, according to Stark, tends to be found at a lower quality university and places little importance on being a future star in their discipline. These students usually still claim a religious identity and attend religious services regularly.[20]

What is interesting about Stark's analysis and conclusions is the explicit interplay between religious identity and professional identity. That is, those students who placed more importance on their religious identity tended to place less importance on their emerging scientist identity, or vice versa. Is this because, as the common assumption goes, it is intellectually untenable to hold onto one's religious identity when taking on the identity of scientist? Or is the issue that as one moves up the prestige ladder within science it becomes socially and culturally untenable to hold onto a religious identity due to issues like stigma? Or is there simply a finite amount of social and cognitive resources that a person can put into maintaining multiple primary identities, so that if one starts to dominate, others tend to get moved to the back burner (or off the stove entirely)?

Another point worth highlighting from Stark's study is the way religion appeared to be connected to the long-term educational and career path of graduate students. The more religious students were in less prestigious universities as a graduate student, but they also tended to have come from less prestigious undergraduate universities. In fact, more recent research has found that religious students tend to choose less elite undergraduate colleges than nonreligious students.[21] Why this is the case is not entirely clear. It is possible that, given their ties to family and community, religious students are less willing to relocate to attend a distant school. Perhaps they simply place less value on the name or ranking of their future college. And, in some cases, they may view such elite colleges as potentially unwelcoming to their religious faith.

The graduate students who completed my survey and participated in interviews were in relatively elite graduate programs. All of them were in the top sixty programs in their respective disciplines. *US News and World Report* ranks over 250 graduate programs in biology, for instance, so the biology students in this book represent roughly the top 25 percent of graduate programs. This means that the religious students in these programs are the exceptions to Stark's typology. With that in mind, to what extent are these students religious?

Affiliations, Beliefs, and Behaviors

My survey of over 1,300 graduate students in five disciplines provides a needed update to Stark's over fifty-year-old survey. Table 1.1 presents the broad religious affiliations of the students who took the survey. Overall, 62 percent of the students are religiously unaffiliated. In the general population of similarly aged and educated adults, the religiously unaffiliated population is 35 percent, so it would appear that graduate students in the sciences are almost twice as likely to be religiously unaffiliated.[22] This unaffiliated percentage is also about twice what Stark found in his study. Given the growth of the religiously unaffiliated in

TABLE 1.1 Current Religious Affiliations of Science Graduate Students

	Current Religious Affiliation
Christian	25%
Jewish	4%
Other	9%
Unaffiliated	62%
Total	*100%*

the general population, it is expected that this growth would also be reflected among graduate students. Examining the unaffiliated percentage more closely, about half of these unaffiliated students (30% of the 62%) identify simply as "not religious." Another 12 percent identify as "agnostic," while 20 percent identify as "atheist."

Christians represent 25 percent of the students overall. This category breaks down into 7 percent who identify as Protestant, 9 percent who identify as Catholic, 6 percent who say they are "just a Christian," 2 percent who identify as Mormon, and 1 percent who identify as Orthodox. Protestants are about double the proportion of Catholics in the general population of similarly aged and educated adults, so the fact that their share of the graduate student population is slightly smaller than Catholics is noteworthy. As noted earlier, this finding of a Protestant gap among Christians in graduate school is similar to what Stark found in his study many years ago.

Overall, Jewish students represent 4 percent of graduate students in these disciplines, while other religions represent 9 percent. The latter category consists of Muslims (1%), Buddhists (1%), Hindus (3%), and a variety of other groups. Compared to Stark's findings, the Jewish category appears to have shrunk among graduate students while the "other religions" category has grown.

Thanks to recent surveys of science faculty, like Ecklund's, one can compare the religious affiliations of graduate students to those of their likely teachers and advisors. Table 1.2 shows the religious affiliations of students in this book alongside the religious affiliations of faculty studied in Ecklund's book. We see that the percentage of Christians is the same among graduate students and faculty, with one in four identifying as Christian. The percentage of Jews is much higher among faculty (16%) than among graduate students (4%). The percentage of graduate students identifying with an "other" religion is fairly close to the faculty percentage (9% versus 7%), while graduate students are slightly more likely to be religiously unaffiliated than faculty (62% versus 52%).

TABLE 1.2 Science Graduate Students' Religious Affiliations as Compared to Faculty Religious Affiliations

	Graduate Students	Faculty (Ecklund 2010)
Christian	25%	25%
Jewish	4%	16%
Other	9%	7%
Unaffiliated	62%	52%
Total	100%	100%

Note: Faculty percentages are from Elaine Howard Ecklund, *Science vs. Religion: What Scientists Really Think* (New York: Oxford University Press, 2010).

The difference between Jewish faculty and students may be due to Jewish graduate students pursuing careers as professors at a higher rate than other students, or it may be due to the faculty representing a different generation of professors. There is some evidence in my data that Jewish students are less likely to pursue careers outside of academia. For example, when asked if they intend to pursue a research career in an industry, government, or nonprofit setting, only 9 percent of Jewish students strongly agreed that they intend to pursue this path, as compared to 25 percent of Christian students who answered the same way.

Religious affiliation is just one aspect of an individual's overall religious life. My survey also asked students about some key religious beliefs and behaviors. Many earlier studies of scientists' religiosity, such as those conducted by Leuba, focused on scientists' belief in God. Table 1.3 presents the responses to this question from the students I surveyed. As shown in the table, 30 percent of science graduate students clearly state that they do not believe in God, while another 28 percent express a more agnostic position, saying they "don't know whether there is a God and [they] don't believe there is a way to find out." A physics student, referencing a quotation from Douglas Adams' novel *The Hitchhiker's Guide to the Galaxy*,[23] told me that he was "a fairy-at-the-bottom-of-the-garden atheist."[24] He explained:

I think if there's a God, it probably exists in the same way that you think that the fairy in the garden makes the plants grow. . . . there may be some underlying mechanism for reality that is hard for us to look at or touch, but it is also hard for me to think of anything existing outside reality.[25]

Looking at the other end of the responses, we find 11 percent of students stating strongly that they do believe in God without any doubt and another 11 percent saying that they generally believe in God but do have some doubts. Mark and Adhira, whom we met at the beginning of this chapter, illustrate this believers group.

The remaining 20 percent of students are between these atheist/agnostic and believer positions, with 15 percent saying that they don't believe in a "personal God" but "do believe in a Higher Power of some kind" and another 5 percent saying that they sometimes believe in God and sometimes do not. A chemistry student I spoke with exemplifies this type of position:

I get conflicted because I like to think that there's a better understanding about the things we don't know. It's so tempting to say, "Yeah, there has to be some higher power because we know all this, and all of this can't be explained completely." I don't know. Yeah, I guess a bit of me is still kind of spiritual.[26]

TABLE 1.3 Belief in God among Science Graduate Students

	Overall
I don't believe in God	30%
I don't know whether there is a God and I don't believe there is any way to find out	28%
I don't believe in a personal God, but I do believe in a Higher Power of some kind	15%
I find myself believing in God some of the time, but not at others	5%
While I have doubts, I feel that I do believe in God	11%
I know God really exists and I have no doubts about it	11%
Total	100%

TABLE 1.4 Science Graduate Students'
Frequency of Religious Service Attendance

	Overall
Never	50%
Less than once a year	13%
Once or twice a year	22%
Once a month	5%
Once a week	8%
More than once a week	2%
Total	*100%*

In sum, when it comes to belief in God, roughly one in five science graduate students are believers, another one in five are what we might call liminal believers, and three in five are atheist or agnostic.[27]

The students who took my survey also reported their frequency of attendance at religious services. As seen in Table 1.4, 50 percent said that they never attend religious services. Another 35 percent attend services very rarely, equating to perhaps once a year. The remaining 15 percent attend fairly regularly, going once a month or more. These three attendance groups correlate fairly strongly with the three belief groups identified above. That is, believers are more likely to attend regularly, liminal believers are more likely to attend rarely, and atheists and agnostics are more likely to never attend.

Despite this apparent correlation, my survey data and interviews found that attendance had a somewhat weaker connection to students' beliefs and personal sense of religiosity, and in part this seems to be related to the disruptions and demands associated with graduate school.[28] One biology student, for instance, told me about how he was primarily engaging with a religious community online because he had not been able to find a community on campus. He explained:

Most of my activity tends to be more on the virtual side rather than on the physical. Mostly because, for one thing, there's no Christian group on campus at this point that I'm aware of, which is saying something for a university of our size. I know there was a small group of religious people that gathered once or twice. I couldn't make their initial schedule, so I don't know what happened to that. I don't see their group on the university website anymore. So I think while there are actual Protestants or whatever groups, I'm not sure how active those things are.[29]

Other students who expressed a belief in God or reported that they were religious similarly mentioned not yet having found a church in their university's community that they liked or simply that they did not have time to attend regularly.

Despite some of the challenges of attending religious series during graduate school, many religious students, like Mark from the beginning of this chapter, are active participants in a religious congregation during their graduate program. A Catholic physics student, for instance, described his and his wife's active participation in a congregation:

We belong to a parish community, where we go to mass once a week at least. And we're also part of the music ministry in the church. I play bass guitar and she sings. We have been involved also with the RCIA (Rite of Christian Initiation of Adults) program there, putting on different talks and what not.[30]

The question, "Independently of whether you attend religious services or not, would you say you are a very religious person, a moderately religious person, a slightly religious person, or not a religious person?" sheds important light on how central and salient a student's religious life is to them.[31] More than stating a belief in God or attending religious services, this question represents the extent to which a student's faith is an important part of their identity.

As seen in Table 1.5, 7 percent of the students I surveyed identify as very religious, 13 percent identify as moderately religious, 14 percent say

TABLE 1.5 Science Graduate Students'
Self-Defined Religiosity

	Overall
Very religious	7%
Moderately religious	13%
Slightly religious	14%
Not a religious person	66%
Total	*100%*

they are slightly religious, and 66 percent identify as not religious. In mapping these percentages to the other questions we have examined, it can be said that about one in five students are fairly religious (i.e., very or moderately religious, believing in God, attending relatively regularly), one in five are marginally religious (i.e., identifying as slightly religious, with a liminal belief in God, and attending rarely), and three in five are nonreligious (i.e., identify as nonreligious, atheist or agnostic, and never attend).

Religiosity and Cultural Affiliation

One pattern that can be seen in the survey data is that Christian students tend to identify as more strongly religious than those holding other affiliations. For instance, 62 percent of Christian students identify as very or moderately religious, as compared to 16 percent of Jewish students and 39 percent of students affiliating with some other religion. Students in the latter two groups often discussed how they viewed their religious affiliation in more cultural terms.

A Jewish sociology student, for instance, told me "I identify as Jewish. I haven't gone to [synagogue] in years, but when I do go, it is just to be around the culture. Even the other Jews that I know will say, 'I only go to this temple because they don't talk about God.' It's all about community."[32] Similarly, a psychology student who states her affiliation as Hindu clarified this in our conversation.

I'm a lot more of a cultural Hindu than I am a religious Hindu . . . I don't feel like I can hold onto my Indian identity without holding onto my Hindu identity because those are so married together. I prayed every night before bed growing up, still celebrate all religious holidays. And it's my way of staying in touch with my family and connecting to them.[33]

For at least some of these students, identifying as culturally religious appeared, in part, to be a way to protect themselves from some of the connotations of being seen as *actually religious*. The Hindu psychology student made this point explicitly, telling me,

I think I have my problems with the identity of what religion means to a number of people. I think personally and internally I can't remove myself from being a religious person, but I wouldn't say as a social identity I would call myself religious because it has so many negative connotations in this day and age. So, I see myself more as spiritual and culturally Hindu.

It is interesting that this idea of being "culturally religious" did not seem to be used by Christian students. The negative connotations of being "actually religious" in the United States, particularly in relation to science, derive largely from stereotypes of Christians. This likely provides less opportunity for Christian students to find this middle ground, as any identification with Christianity is going to come with those negative connotations. Students who identify as Jewish, Muslim, or Hindu, on the other hand, can deflect those connotations by pointing to the cultural basis of their religiosity.

Disciplinary Differences

So far, we have focused on overall religiosity across all of the science graduate students in my study, but there has also always been an interest in differences in religiosity *among* scientists. For example, in his pioneering study, Leuba observed differences in religiosity across scientific disciplines. Specifically, he found that psychologists, sociologists, and biologists were less likely to believe in God, as compared to "physical scientists." Leuba argued that this difference resulted from how these disciplines viewed the world. He wrote,

> Psychologists, sociologists, and biologists in very large numbers recognize fixed orderliness in organic and psychical life, and not merely in inorganic existence; while frequently physical scientists recognize the recognize the presence of invariable law in the inorganic world only. The belief in a personal God . . . is, therefore, less often possible to students of psychical and of organic life than to physical scientists.

In other words, due to the nature of their research, psychologists, sociologists, and biologists tend to view the mind, humans, and society in scientific terms, which limits the role of a supernatural God in these areas. In contrast, physicists' and chemists' scientific lens tends to be applied only to looking at rocks, stars, and other objects outside of the human domain. This, Leuba argues, provides more room for these scientists to isolate their scientific worldview from their religious beliefs.[34]

Other surveys conducted after Leuba's have found similar disciplinary differences. Echoing Leuba's argument, Lehman and Shriver argued in their 1968 study that scientists in fields like physics or chemistry have greater "scholarly distance from religion," as religion is not a direct topic or object of study in these fields. This differs from fields like psychology, where religion can naturally be placed, so to speak, under the microscope.[35]

Focusing more on the differences between the natural and social sciences, others have offered a somewhat different interpretation. The sociologist Robert Wuthnow, for instance, argued that the greater irreligiosity of fields like psychology or sociology is more a function of "posturing" and boundary creation.[36] Because the line between these disciplines and non-science disciplines is blurrier, researchers in these fields try to overcompensate by appearing to be very scientific, which is culturally associated with being very irreligious. Religious physicists, though perhaps seen as odd, are still seen as real scientists. Sociologists, on the other hand, are already on shaky footing when it comes to being seen as scientists, so they may feel it is better not to rock the boat by being religious as well.

More recent research, however, has not found clear differences between the physical and social/life sciences or between the natural and social sciences.[37] In our 2007 analysis, Elaine Howard Ecklund and I found that physicists at elite universities were more likely to say that they do not believe in God than chemists were, but not more likely to say so than biologists, sociologists, or psychologists were.[38]

What does my survey of graduate students find regarding disciplinary differences in religiosity? Table 1.6 shows the self-defined religiosity of the students across disciplines. There are some differences across the disciplines, although not overwhelming in size or clear in implications. On the one hand, psychology and sociology students are the least likely to identify as very religious (5% each), which sort of goes in the direction of the natural versus social distinction some have found in the past. Given those arguments, we might expect that the psychology and sociology students would be the most likely to say they are not religious at all. This is not the case, however, as these students seem instead more likely to be in the slightly religious group. Physics students are actually

TABLE 1.6 Science Graduate Students' Self-Defined Religiosity, by Discipline

	By Discipline				
	Biology	Chemistry	Physics	Psychology	Sociology
Very religious	6%	6%	10%	5%	5%
Moderately religious	11%	19%	11%	10%	13%
Slightly religious	16%	11%	9%	19%	19%
Not a religious person	67%	64%	70%	66%	63%
Total	100%	100%	100%	100%	100%

Note: Design-based F-test (9,522) = 2.26; $p < .05$

the most likely to say they are nonreligious, but are also the most likely to say they are very religious. That is, physics students appear to be a bit more polarized in their religiosity. Overall, though, discipline does not seem to have a particularly large association with graduate student religiosity.

"Greater" versus "Lesser" Scientists-in-Training

In addition to disciplinary differences, there has long been an interest in whether more successful or "greater" scientists are less religious than more ordinary or less successful scientists. Remember that Leuba did find that more elite scientists were less likely to believe in God or the afterlife, and this finding has been reiterated in studies that have followed, including Stark's study of graduate students. Many have interpreted such findings as a sign that these elite scientists' higher level of understanding has eroded their religious faith. Leuba, however, saw this connection as more spurious than causal:

> Greater eminence implies, doubtless, greater knowledge in the field of eminence. . . . But this does not mean that the loss of belief accompanying eminence arises entirely or even chiefly from greater knowledge. The reward of eminence is not usually given for mere knowledge and sheer intellectual ability. . . . The men of higher rank are, on the whole, distinguished among their colleagues for activity, tenacity, and self-reliance. Of these qualities, at least the last two tend to resist the forces of tradition, of authority, and of prestige . . .

In other words, all scientists tend to be quite intelligent and quite knowledgeable about science. Those who are less successful in their careers are not dumb, but rather they do not have certain personality traits, which Leuba labeled tenacity and self-reliance, that lead them to fiercely climb the ladder of the scientific ranks. The personality traits that are beneficial for gaining status in science, according to Leuba, tend to run counter to the traits that might attract people to religion, such as a fondness for tradition and adherence to authority. Based on this, Leuba concluded that "the greater loss of belief suffered by the greater men is probably not to be ascribed chiefly to their greater knowledge, but rather to certain temperamental qualities or energies which make it relatively easy for them to rid themselves of much of the social pressure to which other yield."[39] The last part of this statement is interesting, as Leuba does not seem to see the careerism inherent in becoming a "great scientist" as its own type of social pressure. That is, Leuba interprets this link as mainly a function of having an independent mindset that just so happens to benefit a scientific career and harm one's commitment to religion. It is possible, however, to see this pattern as a shifting of one's identity from one source of meaning and community to another.[40]

Regardless of the question of careerism, is there evidence of a difference in religiosity between "greater" and "lesser" scientists-in-training? Granted, graduate students are just beginning their careers, so it is unlikely that any would be considered "great" or "elite" in a broader sense. There are ways to examine this question, however. We might consider, for instance, whether there are differences in religiosity across the rankings of graduate programs. If we assume that more promising or talented students attend more elite graduate programs, then we might expect that religiosity would be less pervasive in them than in less highly ranked programs. Table 1.7 shows the self-defined religiosity of students across four tiers of programs based on their position in *US News and World Report*'s ranking of graduate programs. The overall picture does not support any differences in religiosity across the rankings of graduate programs, however.[41] We see that 6 percent of students in the top programs, or Tier 1, identify as very religious, as compared to 8 percent in Tier 4, a statistically indistinguishable difference. Looking at the other end of the spectrum, 65 percent of Tier 1 students identify as nonreligious, as compared to 64 percent of Tier 4 students. Again, this is statistically equivalent, which means that the small differences that we see are likely due to chance.

TABLE 1.7 Science Graduate Students' Self-Defined Religiosity, by *US News and World Report* Ranking of Graduate Program

	Tier 1 (1–15)	Tier 2 (16–30)	Tier 3 (31–45)	Tier 4 (46–60)
Very religious	6%	8%	5%	8%
Moderately religious	13%	12%	12%	18%
Slightly religious	16%	14%	14%	10%
Not a religious person	65%	66%	69%	64%
Total	*100%*	*100%*	*100%*	*100%*

Note: Design-based F-test $(7, 440) = 0.86$; $p = .54$ (not significant)

Another approach to answering this question could be to look at the number of research publications a graduate student has produced in their nascent career. Producing peer-reviewed publications is one of the primary metrics that all scientists are judged on, and this judgement begins in graduate school. At least for those students pursuing careers in academic science, a record of publication is seen as a sign of future success by hiring committees, and the expectations surrounding how much graduate students should have published by the end of their programs have increased.[42] In short, today's graduate students with strong publication records might be tomorrow's elite scientists.

My survey asked students to report on the number of articles, solo-authored or co-authored, that they have published or have had accepted for publication in peer-reviewed journals. When we look at the average number of publications for students in each of the self-defined religiosity categories, we find almost no differences. Students who identify as very religious reported an average of 2.0 publications, which is exactly the same as the average for those who identify as moderately religious and slightly religious. Those who identify as nonreligious reported slightly more publications, at an average of 2.3, but this is not statistically different from the other averages (i.e., there is no reason to be confident that the 0.3 gap between the other religiosity categories is due to anything but random chance).[43]

Religious Origins

Asking about the religiosity of scientists naturally leads us to focus on their *current* religious identities, beliefs, and behaviors. But these do not come without any history, of course, and understanding that history provides important context for understanding graduate students' current religious lives. Do science graduate students tend to grow up in religious households, or are they more likely to come from religiously unaffiliated families?

My survey asked students to identify the religion in which they were raised. Table 1.8 shows that most of the students, about four in five, say that they were raised in a religious tradition. Specifically, 60 percent say they were raised Christian, 6 percent were raised Jewish, and 11 percent were raised in some other tradition. As shown earlier, in Table 1.1, this compares to 25 percent currently identifying as Christian, 4 percent identifying as Jewish, and 11 percent identifying with some other religion. In short, there appears to be a large shift of science graduate students who were raised Christian now identifying as unaffiliated.

While this shift is dramatic, it does not necessarily represent a massive change in the actual religiosity of these students. Research examining the growth of the unaffiliated population in general has found that much of this growth has come from individuals who previously claimed a nominal affiliation but were by no means religious in terms of their

TABLE 1.8 Science Graduate Students' Childhood Religious Affiliations

	Childhood Religious Affiliation
Christian	60%
Jewish	6%
Other	11%
Unaffiliated	23%
Total	*100%*

TABLE 1.9 Science Graduate Students'
Self-Defined Childhood Religiosity

	Childhood Religiosity
Very religious	13%
Moderately religious	18%
Slightly religious	20%
Not a religious person	49%
Total	*100%*

strength of belief or religious practice. That is, much of the growth of the unaffiliated population has come simply from people changing the label they place on themselves rather than changing any underlying beliefs or behaviors.[44] Setting labels aside, therefore, how religious were these students when they were children?

Table 1.9 shows students' responses to a question about their level of religiosity at age 16. This question is similar to the current religiosity question presented earlier, in Table 1.5. Comparing childhood religiosity to current religiosity shows some declines, but not as dramatic as those seen in the religious affiliation percentages. Thirteen percent of students say they were very religious as children, as compared to 7 percent who say they are currently very religious. We see similar declines of around 5 or 6 percentage points in the moderately and slightly religious categories. This results in an increase of 17 percent in the percentage of students saying they are nonreligious. This is a significant increase, but much more moderate than the increase seen in the percentage identifying as religiously unaffiliated. In sum, most of the shift to being religiously unaffiliated appears to come from students who were not particularly religious in the first place. For instance, a sociology student I spoke with described himself as an atheist. When I asked about the role of religion in his childhood, he responded fairly indifferently: "I mean, I went to church. I was confirmed as Lutheran. [But] I was not super-religious . . . pretty average for my area. My parents aren't super-religious. . . ."[45]

Focusing on One in Five or Four in Five

We have seen that for about 20 percent of science graduate students, religion is a significant part of their identity and community. These students express belief in God, attend religious services fairly regularly, and consider themselves religious. Religious students, therefore, make up a sizable minority of the population of students training to be scientists. These students are not so rare as to be inconsequential (although it is important to be careful about defining any percentage of people as inconsequential). At the same time, these students may be rare enough to feel isolated or be perceived as unusual by others.

Of course, it is also possible to focus on the four in five students who are not religious in any substantial way. Indeed, the majority of these students do not express any level of belief in God, never attend religious services, and do not identify as a religious person at all. Some observers might be tempted to see these students as confirmation that science has eroded their religiosity by undermining the plausibility of religion's claims concerning specific scientific issues, such as the origin of life, or by undermining the plausibility of broader religious foundations, such as the existence of a God. However, as we have seen, most of these students were only marginally religious to begin with, even if they were raised nominally in some religion. This does not mean that they do not see tensions between religion and science, or that these tensions played no role in their disaffiliation from religion. In the next chapter, I explore these issues and the broader question of how scientists-in-training think about religion, science, and the relationship between the two.

Views on the Religion-Science Relationship

Jessica and Arjun

Jessica, a chemistry graduate student, grew up participating regularly in religion. "We went to a rock-and-roll Jesus church . . . one of those contemporary Christian churches with a worship band and stuff. I sang on the worship team. I volunteered with the four and five-year-olds; we ran Sunday school for them."[1] In talking about her experiences with organized religion, Jessica expressed some ambivalence, particularly in relation to her nascent career in science.

> I remember I was talking to somebody [at church] once, and I was like, "Yeah, I'm looking at colleges." He was like, "You should really check out Liberty University. They have a great program." I was like, "In what?" He said, "In worship leading." I was like, "Hmm." I don't know . . . I've had a really love-hate relationship with church. I had a woman at my church when I went home one time ask me what I was studying. I told her I was studying chemistry, and she was like, "That's sweet, but you know that's not real, right?" I was like, "Girl, you're eighty, so I'm going to let it slide."

Jessica remembered religion being a common topic of conversation at home. Her father, who had a background in engineering, encouraged her to make connections between her interest in science and their family's religious life.

> He would be like, "You have to read *The Case for Christ*." Because it's like an evidence-based approach to looking at why there might be a higher

power and stuff like that, and just different studies. He's always been very interested in science but has always still believed pretty passionately about a higher power existing.

Despite her mixed experiences, Jessica still saw her faith as part of her current and future life.

Right now, I feel like my whole thinking about that has been put toward Parable of the Talents. I'm pretty sure there's a God. I'm pretty sure he's giving me these skills, so I need to cultivate them now, so I can do what I'm supposed to do with them if that makes sense. At this point it doesn't mean necessarily that I need to have to go to church every week. That's just not really in the cards for me at this point, just based on time. I still think about it a lot, though.

There are some parallels between Jessica's experiences with and opinions about the "religion and science" relationship and those of Arjun, a Hindu student pursuing a PhD in physics. Arjun remembered when he began developing an interest in physics.

I was about twelve years old, and we learned Euclidean geometry back then, so there were these circles and cyclic quadrilaterals and all those things. And I really liked that part of it. And then a year later I learned about astrophysics. And that was my favorite subject back then. So I liked applying geometry and finding distances between stops and so on. So I was really fascinated with that subject. That's when I decided that I wanted to do physics.[2]

Arjun's early reading and experiments in physics led him to think explicitly about the dynamic between religion and science.

I would simply pick up some religious stories, some mythological story, and analyze it from a physics perspective. Like, is it really feasible? Is it realistic? Like the description of the story. It's unrealistic because you can do these calculations and show that it's unrealistic. So, when I was a teenager, I was a strong critic of religion, because I could clearly see that none of those things are true.

Arjun described his parents as quite religious, although he said that his father was more invested in the social participation tied to Hindu celebrations and events than the belief components. When he told his father, who had a master's degree in physics, that he had concluded that certain Hindu stories were "unreal because the physical parameters don't agree," his father directed him to an Indian author who had also written about the Hindu mythologies from a scientific perspective.

> He just jokingly said I should maybe read S. L. Bhyrappa's books or contact him. I never took that seriously until I was twenty or twenty-one. And then I started reading books from the same author. And then I read the book that my father had mentioned back when I was thirteen. That was fascinating because that was, I will say that that's one of those events that, helped me understand religion better, not as a version of reality . . . it's not a version of reality and you're to take it in a different way. And reading those books I think helped me in that process.

What struck me in speaking with Jessica and Arjun is the way "religion and science" had woven itself throughout their lives in a very personal and complex way. Discussions about the relationship between religion and science are often dominated by either highly intellectualized takes provided by theologians or historians, or highly ideological takes provided by some public scientists and religious leaders. For Jessica and Arjun, on the other hand, the religion–science relationship is not some abstract debate, but something that has influenced their personal relationships and professional itineraries.

How do scientists-in-training perceive the religion–science relationship? How does their religiosity (or lack thereof) influence those perceptions? How has students' religiosity affected their views on science, and how has their exposure to science affected their views on religion? These are the questions I explore in this chapter.

Conflict, Collaboration, or Independence?

In his definitive book *Religion and Science*, the physicist and philosopher Ian Barbour argued that the myriad historical, philosophical, and theological arguments about the relationship between religion and science can be boiled down to a few fundamental positions.[3] The first—the position that often dominates the conversation—is that religion and science are in perpetual conflict, inherently at odds. The nature of this conflict is typically said to result from competing claims about the nature of reality and the legitimate paths to understanding that reality. Many religious people, for instance, view the world as having the potential for miracles and divine intervention. In contrast, some scientists, such as Richard Dawkins, have argued that "If ever there was a slamming of the door in the face of constructive investigation, it is the word miracle. . . . Once you buy into the position of faith, then suddenly you find yourself losing all your natural skepticism and your scientific—really scientific— credibility."[4] In other words, as a biology student who describes herself as nonreligious told me, "religion is the ball and chain of science."[5]

The second position identified by Barbour is that religion and science are independent of each other. Writers who have taken this position generally argue that religion and science have no reason to conflict with each other because their purposes are fundamentally different. Perhaps the most eloquent example of this position was offered by the late paleontologist and evolutionary biologist Stephen Jay Gould. In evaluating the religion–science relationship, Gould offered the concept of *nonoverlapping magisteria*:

> No such conflict [between religion and science] should exist because each subject has a legitimate magisterium, or domain of teaching

authority—and these magisteria do not overlap (the principle that I would like to designate as NOMA, or "nonoverlapping magisteria").

The net of science covers the empirical universe: what is it made of (fact) and why does it work this way (theory). The net of religion extends over questions of moral meaning and value. These two magisteria do not overlap, nor do they encompass all inquiry (consider, for starters, the magisterium of art and the meaning of beauty).

To cite the arch clichés, we get the age of rocks, and religion retains the rock of ages; we study how the heavens go, and they determine how to go to heaven.[6]

The third position for the religion–science relationship identified by Barbour is collaboration.[7] Individuals who have taken a collaborative view of religion and science argue that the two are neither in conflict nor irrelevant to each other. At the very least, some argue, science and religion benefit when their institutions and leaders engage in dialogue on moral and social issues of interest to one or both. Others have argued that scientific knowledge and discoveries can enhance religious faith by revealing the work of God, and that religious faith can motivate and inspire scientific discoveries by providing a desire to understand God's work. Greg Cootsona, who has led several major projects designed to engage religious congregations in conversations about science, illustrates this sentiment:

> Because I believe Jesus is Lord of all, I'm committed to grasping and cel-
> ebrating the beautiful intricacy of the created order (which, according to
> Psalm 19, declares God's glory). So, if science can truly uncover truth about
> the world, we should embrace those discoveries. Our faith might be chal-
> lenged, but more often, I've discovered, it is enhanced. Indeed, one reason I
> came to love studying science, after being a lifelong student of literature and
> theology, is the amazing way scientific discoveries strengthen my faith.[8]

Although the independence and collaboration orientations have had some prominent advocates, and historians of science have largely rejected the conflict orientation,[9] the "religion-science warfare" narrative has long dominated the public sphere and popular culture. For whatever reason, voices advocating for the conflict narrative have tended to be louder and stories of conflict have tended to be seen as more interesting or marketable. Watching Bill Nye, "the science guy," debate the well-known creationist Ken Ham apparently makes for better live Tweeting and news headlines.[10]

The cultural dominance of the conflict narrative is even more curious considering that surveys have shown that the majority of the US public does not view religion and science as being in conflict with each other. A few years ago, Elaine Howard Ecklund and I surveyed a representative sample of over ten thousand American adults and asked them how they personally viewed the relationship between religion and science. Only 27 percent said that they saw religion and science as being in conflict with each other. This group was fairly evenly split between those who said they were "on the side of science" and those who said they were "on the side of religion" within this conflict. The idea that religion and science are independent from each other was chosen by 35 percent of respondents, while the collaboration idea was endorsed by 38% of respondents.[11] Analyses of other surveys have found similar patterns.[12]

Of course, scientists may differ from the average US adult in their views on the religion–science relationship. The best data on this question come from another study led by Elaine Howard Ecklund. In a survey of over 1,700 academic scientists in the US, she found that 29 percent of scientists endorsed the conflict narrative, and all of these individuals said that they were "on the side of science." So, overall, scientists do not appear to be more pro-conflict than the average US adult, but those who endorse the conflict position are much more homogenously on the pro-science side. A majority of scientists in Ecklund's survey, at 51 percent, said that they viewed religion and science as having an independent relationship, which makes this a more popular narrative among scientists than the general public. On the other hand, only 12 percent chose the

TABLE 2.1 Science Graduate Students' Views on the Religion-Science Relationship Overall, and by Current Self-Defined Religiosity

"For me personally, my understanding of science and religion can be described as a relationship of . . ."	Overall	By Current Religiosity			
		Very Religious	Moderately Religious	Slightly Religious	Not a Religious Person
Conflict-On the side of religion	<1%	4%	0%	<1%	<1%
Conflict-On the side of science	28%	<1%	1%	12%	40%
Independence	49%	13%	43%	67%	50%
Collaboration	22%	83%	59%	21%	10%
Total	100%	100%	100%	100%	100%

Note: Design-based F-test (6, 364) = 49.07; p <.001

collaboration narrative, suggesting that scientists are less comfortable with this model than the general public.

How do graduate students in science perceive the religion and science relationship? I asked the students who took my survey the same question used in these past studies to see how they compare to the US public and to more established academic scientists. As seen in the overall column of Table 2.1, the scientists-in-training in my sample were fairly close to the scientists in Ecklund's sample in their views of the religion-science relationship. About 28 percent of the students said that they see this relationship as one of conflict, and almost all of these students are on the side of science. Just under half of the students, at 49 percent, said that they see religion and science as being independent from each other, and 22 percent said that they view religion and science as having a collaborative relationship.

These responses do not significantly differ across the five scientific disciplines represented by the graduate students in my survey. However, as seen in Table 2.1, there are some differences across levels of religiosity. Students who are not religious at all, for instance, are more likely to favor the conflict narrative and less likely to favor the collaboration narrative. Interestingly, the conflict narrative loses much of its popularity even among students who only describe themselves as slightly religious. These slightly religious students are especially drawn to the independence narrative. Among moderately and very religious students, however, we start to see a shift toward the collaboration narrative.

In sum, there seem to be three types of graduate students when it comes to perceptions of the religion and science relationship. Nonreligious students are more likely to embrace the idea that religion and science are in conflict. Marginally religious students are less comfortable with the conflict narrative, but do not see religion and science as needing each other. More religious students, however, do not see such an independent relationship as tenable or desirable and would like to see a more collaborative relationship between religion and science.

Identity Signaling

It is tempting to see responses to a survey question on the religion–science relationship as a product of an intellectual process, in which individuals' responses are based on some assessment of evidence and arguments about how religion and science do or should relate to each other. This assumption is appealing to those who disagree with differing responses, as it allows them to believe that everyone would agree with them if presented with the same evidence.

There are undoubtedly intellectual processes underlying such survey responses, as many of the graduate students I spoke with have spent significant time reading and thinking about the religion and science relationship. But we should also see these responses as being fueled by social and psychological processes. In other words, how an individual perceives the religion–science relationship often says as much about how they view themselves as it does about how they see religion and science.

In reflecting on his finding that African Americans and individuals of lower socioeconomic status tend to be more likely to say that there is conflict between religion and science and that they are "on the side of religion," sociologist Joseph Baker argued that it is these groups' historical and contemporary exclusion from the institution of science that leads them to see science and scientists as a social and cultural "other." Declaring that they are on the opposing team in some conflict with science allows such individuals to express a sense of membership in a group outside of science.[13]

When viewed in this light, the desire of very religious graduate students to see collaboration between religion and science is understandable. This is not because they have unique evidence or information on the religion-science dynamic, but rather because religion and science are both major contributors to their own identities and to their sense of belonging in larger communities. For these students, it is not possible to split religion and science from each other any more than it is possible to split their own identity in two. They cannot see religion and science as being at war with each other, as this would mean that their own sense of self is experiencing some internal conflict. In short, highly religious students are on both team science and team religion, so endorsing collaboration between religion and science is an expression of those identities.

Looking at the other end of the spectrum, expressions of conflict between religion and science can also be a way for students, particularly nonreligious students, to signal their own identities and desired membership in a group. This explains, in part, why students who identify explicitly as an "atheist" are more likely (58.2%) than those who identify as "agnostic" (33.9%) or simply as "not religious" (30.2%) to say that they see religion and science as being in conflict. Studies have highlighted the important role that science plays as an identity construct for atheists, often explicitly in relation to religion.[14] Put differently, those who identify as atheist often point to science and its supposed conflict with religion as being important to how they think of themselves and the communities with which they affiliate. It is not that atheist students have necessarily thought more about the religion–science relationship than nonreligious students who identify as agnostic or as nonreligious (or religious students). Nor do students identifying as atheist necessarily have unique information about the religion–science relationship. Rather, students identifying as atheist see conflict between religion and science as an important component of how they view themselves. Without that sense of conflict, their own sense of identity and community loses some of its meaning.

Students' Views

Complex social and psychological dynamics underlie a student's decision to choose one response on a survey over another. The bigger issue, however, might be that it is difficult to fully represent an individual's views on the religion–science relationship in a single multiple-choice answer. This is especially true for the religious students I spoke with, who had often thought deeply about these issues and what they meant for their own religious and scientific identities over the course of their lives. Indeed, my conversations with scientists-in-training highlighted just how nuanced many of their views were.

Views on Conflict

Some religious students I spoke with recognized that religion and science could conflict, but this was usually because people were, in their opinions, misusing religion. One such student I met is David, a Christian studying biology. In addition to his scientific interests, David also had an academic interest in philosophy and identified as both a scientist and philosopher. Possibly because of his unique hybrid of interests, David had thought quite a lot about the religion–science relationship. While he did not personally see conflict between religion and science, he recognized that some individuals or communities might:

> There's definitely a decent chunk of people in some religious communities I've been a part of who think that what makes a religion important is explaining how the world works, and I don't agree with that. Or, as a scientist, I've realized that in general that's not really true.

Nobody thinks you're supposed to figure out how the sun works from the Bible. Or, at least no real theologians do. But a decent amount of people on the ground sometimes do think, "Well, I read this one passage and I think what it means is this and that means we need to think this about how the world actually works." And it's like no, no you don't.[15]

The idea that the religion-science conflict only arises if one views religion in a "literal" way came up across many of my conversations with students. A chemistry student described his experience when a family member expressed such a view:

I have an uncle who is one of the ones who believes that the Earth is, like, eight thousand years old, and fossils were probably put there to test us or some bullshit. But, I mean, that's clearly at odds with what science indicates and tells us about the universe.

I mean, there's no, outside of, like, the Bible, there's nothing to indicate the world's eight thousand years old. Nothing to tell you that. And holding onto this belief in the face of what we can actually learn and measure about the universe is stupid.[16]

Natalie, a Christian PhD student in psychology, explained to me that she did not personally see science as being in conflict with her religion because she did not adhere to such a literal view:

The relationship with God is more important than this is what happened in this chapter of the Bible. I actually see that as more of a metaphorical thing, I'm more of these stories mean something for how we operate in our lives versus these stories are factual and exactly what happened. I think that makes the conflict not as strong. You can prove whatever you want to, you can prove that this didn't happen in seven days and it doesn't matter because the meaning behind it doesn't get diminished.

As Natalie highlighted, the students I spoke with did not see non-literal approaches to religion as less powerful or meaningful.

The idea that religion-science conflict is actually isolated to particular forms of religion and specific scientific issues that seemingly threaten those specific forms of religion has some basis in research findings. For instance, analyses of national survey data show that individuals who say they view the Bible literally are significantly more likely to perceive conflict between religion and science, as compared to those with more flexible or skeptical views.[17] Moreover, even for literalists, the perception of conflict is limited to a narrow number of scientific issues, most notably the origins of humans and the universe (i.e., creation). These are the issues in which scientific claims appear to some religious individuals as threatening the potential for an active God and the sacredness of humanity.[18]

Other students I interviewed recognized the potential for there to be conflict between religion and science, but saw this conflict as resulting more from religion and science being pulled into political conflicts. In fact, historical and sociological analyses have observed increasing politicization of both religion and science over the past several decades. On the side of religion, the political mobilization of American evangelicals in response to issues concerning (but not limited to) sexuality and abortion in the 1960s and 1970s led to the most visible representations of religion in America being increasingly aligned with political conservatism and, more specifically, the Republican Party.[19] As being religious became increasingly equated with being Republican, the more politically liberal started to identify as religiously unaffiliated.[20]

At the same time, scientists also became increasingly engaged in issues of policy and politics. Some of this involvement began in mundane ways, such as scientists being looked to for advice on shaping programs and regulations to address a wide range of issues, from water quality to poverty reduction. Scientists' involvement in such efforts was motivated by their perceived expertise and non-partisan nature. Ironically, though, scientists' involvement in these efforts often weakened their perceived authority, as they became vulnerable to the inevitable political nature of such processes and decisions.[21]

On top of this more indirect involvement in the political realm, some scientists and science organizations became more overtly political. The Union of Concerned Scientists, for instance, was founded in 1969 at the height of the Vietnam War to advocate for "scientific research to be directed away from military technologies and toward solving pressing environmental and social problems."[22] In response to science's real or perceived alignment with the regulatory state and issues seen as liberal issues, political conservatives have become less confident in the scientific community.[23] Similarly, religious conservatives have become increasingly skeptical of and opposed to the role of scientists in policymaking, at least on issues of social and moral concern to them.[24]

Many of the students I interviewed expressed an interest in extending their emerging expertise into the realm of policy and politics. A physics student told me, "I think science should play a bigger role [in society] than it does . . . stuff like the anti-vaccine movement or the anti-GMO movement, or the climate hoax movement, or the flat-earthers, or all this stuff that is, I think, painfully obvious."[25] Similarly, a biology student argued, "I think scientists really need to start being more involved in politics, policy, local issues, because we are considered some of the smartest people in our society, and yet we all live in this bubble where we don't talk to a lot of laymen out there."[26]

Despite their interest, students recognized that such engagement would likely lead to conflicts with religious groups and individuals, although they tended to see science as being less culpable in such conflicts. The biology-philosophy student, David, said, "In my opinion the conflict in the scientific community and the religious community is political in origin, and it started from the religious end, not the scientific end."[27] Eva, a PhD student in psychology, explained her frustration with such conflicts or, more specifically, her frustration with the use of religion, rather than science, in policy making.[28]

I think on a sociopolitical realm there is a total ignoring of science under the basis of religion. Like, "I'm making all of these decisions because the Bible says it," even though we can point to studies done by, like, literally every person that shows that there's climate change, that shows that we should not be restricting abortion rights, that jail doesn't work, that welfare is good, all of these things. But then, science doesn't help with that, because there's a religious basis or a moral right and wrong that people are holding onto and they bring that up higher than science.

Independence

As noted earlier, half of the students in my survey said they viewed science and religion as independent of each other. Some students argued that science is simply not capable of speaking to the validity of religion's most important claims, such as the existence of a God. As a result, they see no potential for conflict regarding those important claims. Alyssa, a Muslim student pursuing a PhD in chemistry, explained her view of this to me:

So I just hold religion as something separate from science, right? That's what they teach you even in middle school. They're like, "Science is about things that you can test and understand. Religion is about things that you can't test in order to understand them." So in that way I see it as separate.

People will make the argument, "Well, we can explain the universe empirically so we don't need a God, so why would we come up with that?" So the thing is, yes I don't need a God per se to explain the world, in that I believe that things are empirically understandable. When you investigate why something has happened, what the causes are, you can trace that back through physical process.

But even though I was very comfortable with the idea of there not being a God, that doesn't necessarily mean that's true. Just the same way that a lot of atheists will say, "Well, just because you believe in a God, or you want there to be a God, just because you want that doesn't make it true." Well, just because you're not searching for it or don't want it, also doesn't make it not true. What you want has no bearing on the reality of a God or no God.

But you can't argue that there's no God because [you] don't feel like there is, or there is a God because I feel like there is. I mean, that's not something you can argue about. I see that as a totally separate issue. Yes, the world is understandable through physical means, but just because it's understandable through physical means doesn't preclude the idea of there being a God.[29]

Note that Alyssa's argument is different from Stephen Jay Gould's argument about non-overlapping magisteria. Gould argued that religion is concerned with questions of morality and values, not questions of physical processes, and in that sense the two are independent of each other. We might refer to this as "independence-by-function." Alyssa, however, did not necessarily restrict religion to questions of morality. Rather, she saw religion as simply operating outside of normal physical processes that science is capable of understanding. We might call this "independence-by-faith."

Other well-known scientists have advanced this sort of argument. Francis Collins—the former director of the National Institutes for Health—has argued that "There will never be a scientific proof of God's existence. Science explores the natural, and God is outside of the natural. So there is going to be no substitute for making a decision to believe, and that decision will never be undergirded by absolute data-driven proof."[30] Other students I spoke with expressed a similar independence-by-faith sentiment. A psychology student, for instance, told me what she thought about the idea that everything can be explained by science:

I don't think that it is possible [to explain everything with science]; I think religion is based on faith and if you're trying to take all the faith out of it it's not really religion. . . . That's part of what keeps me on the religious side, is that there are many things in religion you can't explain, there's also things in science that can't be explained by science and until that moment I keep a little bit of faith as well.[31]

Gould's argument for independence-by-function was mentioned in some of my conversations with scientists-in-training. David, the biologist-philosopher, explained how he views religion as having a necessary moral function that science cannot provide:

> I think there's something inherently futile about trying to decide what's important by looking at the world. Because I think the other thing I learned from studying evolution is that what's good and what's right and what's important doesn't really always happen.
>
> I don't think there's anything in science to show that [what's right, good, or important]. So I think that's part of why I'm religious. I think if you're a really consistent, really logically rigorous scientist, there's a lot of things you would do that would just be awful, they'd be horrible and everyone knows that and everybody suggests it. But that is what you would have to think if you were really rigorous about saying, "I'm going to decide how I ought to live based on how the world is." I think there's more than that. I think that's what I think of religion as [providing].[32]

A Catholic psychology student expressed a similar sentiment concerning the role of religion as a moral resource that complements the functions of science:

> Priests are not necessarily men of science. The church should not be telling us what we scientifically believe. That's why we have research and science to tell us. These are complementary worlds that can absolutely coexist . . . These are parables and metaphors that are used to, through the different apostles, speak to different groups of people because different

groups of people respond to them in different ways. And that's the way the Bible was written . . . to be morally enlightening.[33]

While many of the religious students I spoke with had thought deeply about the relationship between religion and science, some students simply did not see this as a significant concern. These students saw religion and science as being independent from each other primarily because they were personally indifferent about their relationship. A Muslim physics student, for instance, told me,

> I just don't really think about those things. I believe in something; it doesn't need to be proven. It doesn't need evidence for it to be right. I just believe in it. It doesn't need to be right or wrong. I don't know. I believe it's right, and that's what I believe, and it has nothing to do with my work. I don't try to attribute, for example, any scientific discovery to my religious background or anything like that. I feel like it really doesn't matter. It's not going to make me less religious nor is it going to make going make me more scientific, so to speak. They are completely separate issues or perspectives. There's no connection at all in my experience. I don't connect them. I go practice my religion, and never think about science, and I go practice science and never think about religion. That's it.[34]

Views on Collaboration

In a 2019 *New York Times* op-ed, Dr. David DeSteno, a professor of psychology, argued that "science can learn from religion" in a number of ways. He points to how certain religious beliefs and practices, such as meditation and ritualistic religious behaviors, can inspire scientific hypotheses and interventions for "combating addiction, increasing exercise, saving money and encouraging people to help those in need."[35] The idea that religion and science could inspire each other, and work together, might strike some as an unusual or even controversial claim. However, many of the religious students I interviewed did see religion and science as influencing each other, either at the institutional level or within the students' own life.

Arjun, the physics student who was introduced at the start of this chapter, had a particularly interesting view concerning the role that religion plays in scientific discovery. He viewed religion as providing society a sense of security that has allowed science to take risks:

> I think that religion is necessary for scientific progress. Science is basically exploration outside of what you're comfortable with. By definition, there is an inherent risk in exploration. There's a risk of not finding anything when you go up for an exploration, there's a risk of physical harm or other dangers, especially when you do space exploration and other things. And therefore human beings have to learn how to take risks. If you're a perfectly rational person, why would you ever take a risk? So now you have to convince some small subset of society to take risks. Otherwise you won't make any progress or make any progress in science and technology if you don't take risks and if you don't explore it out into the areas that we're not confronted with. So how do you do that? Well, you have to give them a sense of security by having a certain set of imaginations. So that I think is the broader role that religion plays that you kind of make people feel safer so that they can go and take out, go out and take risks. And that I believe is the connection between religion and science.

Greg, a Jewish sociology PhD student who went through a period of "militant atheism" earlier in his life, told me about how he now sees religion as providing a way of humanizing science.

> The role that religion plays for me is as a guiding structure, and also an aesthetic structure for thoughts and feelings that I think are fairly universal, or are universally accessible to humans. And then seeing the potential for religion to bring people together and create community to think about and discuss our obligations to each other and to the world and to

justice, that was really attractive to me. So that brought me [back] into Judaism . . .

Just to give an example. . . . Love is really important to people, but we don't have this hyper rational positivist understanding of love the way that we engage in it in our daily lives. Because you could break down love and you could say, "Love is just biochemical reactions that have something to do with evolutionary psychology," but all that would be doing is attempting to denigrate something by breaking it into smaller parts, which is something that a certain kind of science often tries to do to the world.

I think that that's a dangerous aspect of science, actually. I think it can be used to de-humanize. Literally, if you want to de-humanize someone and so you speak about them in terms of just physically what they are, and reducing them to just physical phenomena, then you can get rid of the sense of importance of that person as a living being with a consciousness. I think science often tries to do that to the world. . . .

[But,] if you focus on our interconnection, if you focus on spiritual truths, that leads you to conclusions that are fundamentally healthier.[36]

Like Greg, most of the students I spoke with described collaboration between religion and science in personal terms. Several students talked about how they saw religion as motivating their scientific endeavors. A chemistry student told me that,

For me, as a Christian, I feel like [religion does influence science] because of how I connect science to my faith, and the idea that part of honoring and worshiping God is learning about the world that he created, and so for me that's part of science, and that is part of my religious faith, is the idea of actually studying the world.[37]

Other religious students spoke about how they saw science as strengthening their religious faith. A Christian biology student, for example, explained this to me:

I just feel like the more I learn about science and some of the intricacies of how life works, then the more connected I feel to my religion because it is, to me kind of a sign that God exists that all of these things can happen in sync so well.[38]

Similarly, a Muslim chemistry student described to me how learning about and working in science is "just like repeated reminders that there's so much about this world that we don't understand. And we've been trying and trying for all of our history, and we still have no idea. That, for me, is just a pretty powerful thing in reinforcing how amazing God's creation is."[39]

Other students saw religion and science as mutually reinforcing. A Christian physics student told me, "Honestly I think in a lot of ways faith can really accentuate a love for science. And I think science can do the same for making you want to pursue faith more strongly."[40]

Science Undermining or Bolstering Religion

The idea that an individual's scientific research could bolster their religious faith runs counter to the common assumption that exposure to science undermines religious faith. Yet, as the students above highlight, some individuals do find that scientific exploration and knowledge strengthens their religiosity. This is not to say that every religious student I spoke with felt this way. In fact, several students who otherwise described themselves as at least somewhat religious explained to me that their studies and work in science had made them take a more "critical" or analytical eye toward their faith.

One physics student, for instance, told me that science had made him less likely to accept things uncritically:

Especially if I see something that seems to contradict the Bible. [I want to . . .] look at all the archaeology, look at the history, look at the accuracy of the writings, look at what they were trying to say, and through that trying to piece it together. Because within the realm of the Christian, there should be nothing in science, if God created it all, there's nothing in science that should contradict the Bible. Because if God made it then it's not going contradict. And so, I don't want to blindly accept, and I don't want to blindly dismiss anything without trying to figure it out.[41]

A chemistry student expressed a similar sentiment in explaining how science has made him view religion more through the lens of the scientific method. "I feel like some of that [scientific method] has translated over to my personal religion as well. That scientific mindset has kind of contributed some to my approach to religion, and looking at things in that way of trying to just figure out how things go in that."[42]

Note that for both of these students, viewing their faith more "critically" or "scientifically" does not mean that they view themselves as less religious. Some of the students I spoke with, though, did attribute a loss of some or all of their religiosity to science. A different chemistry student, for instance, told me, "I grew up in religious family. Once I started pursuing science, I started questioning everything and no one had an answer. So I started doubting what anyone else would say without proof, and then basically science made me become an atheist."[43]

On the other hand, I also met a couple of students who said that their work in science had moved them away from a strong atheist position and toward a view that is at least somewhat open to or at least sympathetic toward religion. Eva, a psychology student we met earlier, described to me how she was raised Catholic but does not really consider herself religious now. But she notes that she is actually much more open to religion now after a period where she was "very atheist":

I think in my neuroscience research there was a long time where I struggled with trying to make sense of religion and what I study. Everything seemed so deterministic, or nature versus nurture, whatever. There was no space for religion in what I was doing.

I feel like, if anything, the more I've gotten into this work the more I realize, "Oh, we really know nothing and there is really no . . . there would be no way to write off . . . You can't point to science and write off religion," as opposed to in undergrad and in high school where you'd read Richard Dawkins or Malcolm Gladwell and just be like, "This explains all of humanity." And then you're just like, "No, this is not . . . this is not it."[44]

One of the questions my survey of graduate students asked was "Would you say that your knowledge and training in your discipline has made you more religious, had no effect on how religious you are, or made you less religious?" As seen in the overall column of Table 2.2, 63 percent of the student respondents said that their scientific training has had no effect on their religiosity. Of those who say there has been an effect on their religiosity, 28 percent said that science has made them less religious, and 9 percent said that it has made them more religious.

Of course, how religious a student was to begin with is going to affect responses to this question, as we can see in the other columns that show students' responses broken out by how religious they said they were growing up. Those who said they were not religious growing up are more likely to said that science has had no effect on their religiosity, with 78 percent of these students providing this response. This likely

TABLE 2.2 Effect of Scientific Training on Religion, Overall and by Self-Defined Religiosity at Age 16

"Would you say that your knowledge and training in your discipline has . . ."	Overall	By Religiosity at Age 16			
		Very Religious	Moderately Religious	Slightly Religious	Not a Religious Person
Made you more religious	9%	24%	15%	10%	3%
Had no effect on how religious you are	63%	45%	46%	54%	78%
Made you less religious	28%	31%	39%	36%	19%
Total	100%	100%	100%	100%	100%

Note: Design-based F-test (5, 267) = 19.01; p <.001

represents a type of floor effect, in that these students have always seen themselves at the bottom of the religiosity spectrum, and science cannot really push them any further down in the first place. Looking at the other end of the spectrum, though, 45 percent of students who said they were very religious growing up said that science has had no effect on their religiosity. The remaining students who grew up very religious are fairly evenly split between those who said that science has made them more religious (24%) and those that said science has made them less religious (31%). We have seen illustrations of all these groups in the voices of the students presented above.

Moving beyond the Usual Questions

When thinking about "religion and science" among scientists, our minds tend to jump to some standard questions. Are scientists religious? How does science affect their religiosity? How do scientists view the religion–science relationship? These are naturally interesting questions that we have explored in the past two chapters. Yet religion and science influence the lives of scientists, or in this case, scientists-in-training, in more social and psychological ways beyond these usual questions. The next three chapters examine how religion affects the everyday lives of graduate students in the sciences, as well as their future goals in science.

3

Stigma and Hostility

Emily

Emily was an advanced student in a biology PhD program. Her research focused on plant biology. In reflecting on her interest in plants, she pointed to gardening with her father as a child. She also recounted attending an influential science camp:

> It's actually kind of funny. I don't know if it was middle school or high school, but my parents for an unexplainable reason decided to ship my sister and I off to a plant pathology camp. I don't know where they found that. We were the only people there who were not part of their school class that attended, but it was really awesome.[1]

Emily pointed to some common challenges in graduate school:

> I think the most challenging aspect has been a combination of imposter syndrome . . . just trying to make sure that I'm doing the right thing and know what I'm doing and that kind of thing. But, yeah, also just stress and time management, that's a major hurdle that I'm just constantly dealing with.

To her surprise, though, Emily's identity as a Christian had also been a source of stress and conflict in graduate school:

> I was actually really shocked [when I started graduate school] because I've always had atheist friends, and we've always had really good conversations

about religion and respected each other. I was really shocked at the lack of respect of my fellow students as well as professors, just making offhand comments. It was surprising. Yeah, it was. I definitely thought . . . I still feel like I need to hide that part [of my life]. I don't talk about it very much. Maybe there are more people who are religious around me. But I don't feel willing to open up, and maybe they don't either for the same reason.

Emily told me that she feels "completely isolated in this category" and was searching for a social community in graduate school.

I definitely feel like I need to make more of an effort to find friends that have the same beliefs as me. I have plans of finding a church or a study group or a Bible study group or something like that to find friends. I definitely am keeping my eyes and ears out for people who mention religion. I definitely want to find an environment that's supportive. Not everyone has to have the same beliefs, but they have to be respectful of each other.

Religious graduate students in the sciences might not be as rare as some would assume, but they are definitely in the minority. As Emily's experience indicates, holding an identity that is significant to you but is not to those around you can be difficult. Just as it is natural to seek out relationships with people who share common interests and beliefs, it is also natural to feel isolated and frustrated when those relationships are lacking.

It can be especially challenging when the people around you not only do not share an important aspect of your life, but also view that aspect of your life as silly or even antithetical to their own identity. Many religious graduate students in the sciences, like Emily, experience hostility toward their religion from their fellow students, faculty, or the scientific community. In response, some religious students, like Emily, conceal their religious lives, which only serves to increase their isolation by making it difficult for religious science students to find each other. These issues all negatively impact the experiences of religious students in graduate school.

Minorities in Science

The issues religious graduate students in the sciences face are not unique. Much research has documented the experiences of other minority groups in science, particularly women and racial and ethnic minorities.[2] Studies have shown that the predominant cultural image of a scientist is that of a white male,[3] and students who do not fit this image often encounter implicit or explicit messages that they are inherently less capable in science, which can lead them to question their own abilities.[4] Women and racial minorities may look at their peers and faculty, who largely do not look like them, and question whether they truly belong in science.[5] Nor, of course, is science free of the sexism and racism that exists throughout society. These dynamics often lead many women and racial minorities to abandon their initial aspirations in science at some point in their educations or careers.[6]

My own survey documented some of the negative experiences gender and racial minority students face in their science programs. Eighty-three percent of the women in my survey reported that they have had at least one experience of being treated with less respect as a graduate student because of their gender.[7] Similarly, 89 percent of Black students and 74 percent of Latino students report at least one experience of being treated with less respect as a graduate student because of their race or ethnicity.[8]

While these issues are well documented in regard to gender and race, much less attention has been paid to them when it comes to religious graduate students in science. Yet many of the same dynamics apply.

Assumed Atheism

The minority status of religious scientists-in-training combined with the often-invisible nature of their religiosity creates an environment in which an assumption of universal atheism can dominate the culture of science graduate programs.[9] This is in contrast to what is arguably an assumption of religiosity in the larger American social context.[10]

This assumed atheism was recognized not only by many of the religious students I spoke with, but also by several of the nonreligious students I interviewed. When I asked a nonreligious chemistry student how religion comes up in informal conversations in his program, he told me, "I mean, for the most part, I think everyone is basically agnostic or atheist. We sometimes talk about philosophy, but no one talks about their religion or anything."[11] Similarly, a biology student who grew up Christian but no longer identifies with a religion said, "I think that if [religion] does come up, it's not so much as a discussion . . . it's kind of an accepted assumption that everyone in the room is not religious. I think that's the assumption."[12]

Some of the nonreligious students I spoke with seemed to question whether their assumptions about the religious composition of their colleagues were accurate. When I asked an atheist physics student whether he knew of any religious students or faculty in his department, he said, "I think as a whole we are fairly agnostic and those of us who aren't agnostic probably don't tell us, you know. So, I think if they're out there, I'm not sure I know. I'm not sure that they would have told me if they're religious or particularly spiritual."[13] The student appears to recognize that if religious students are part of his school community, there is a good chance they would be hesitant to reveal it.

The biology student mentioned above was only able to think of one example of encountering a religious person as part of her graduate school work. She recounted that

> I had one undergraduate researcher for whom [religion] was very important, and we had some really good conversations about it. I'm sure she brought it up initially, but it was also sort of part of how she viewed her daily life. It came up a lot. But I think she may be the only person that I know for sure, but I would guess there's more. But it is kind of interesting that I don't know [of more religious individuals].[14]

While only able to point to one example of encountering a religious individual in the course of her scientific work, this student questioned whether there could have been more she was not aware of.

Religious students I spoke with also perceived this assumption of atheism within their graduate programs. When I asked a religious student in physics how religion came up in his program, he told me,

> there is this common idea that everyone in the group, probably doesn't believe in God, because it never comes up in any of the socializations that we're having. And in particular, you think of scientists, "yeah they're rationalist. They don't have these sorts of things." So probably no one else in the room believes in God.[15]

In some cases, religious students accepted this assumed atheism as fact. A psychology student stated with confidence that, "I'm almost certain I'm the only religious student in my program."[16] Of course, in a graduate program with over seventy students it is unlikely that this student's perception is accurate. But because this assumed atheism is taken for granted, it is difficult for religious students to start a conversation about their faith, since they assume that no one else cares or understands. This, in turn, makes it difficult to identify and make connections to peers who are also religious.

Negative Comments and Climate

One consequence of this assumed atheism is that it creates an environment where some nonreligious individuals believe it acceptable to be openly hostile or disparaging toward religion. A nonreligious physics student told me, "I know people who do believe. We usually try not to be mocking in front of them."[17] Yet many of the religious students I spoke with did describe comments and interactions that they saw as mocking toward their faith in particular or religion in general. A Christian physics student, for instance, when asked how religion comes up informally among other students and faculty, explained it to me:

> Sometimes maybe people assume that the default religion for a scientist is an atheist or agnostic and that's the preferred manner of speaking, and I would say that doesn't sit well with me, but that's just some people. Some people definitely don't hold religion in high esteem . . . sometimes there are comments that come out that way.

Although this student seems to brush off the negative comments by adding that "most people are respectful," it is also clear that those negative comments have made an impression on him.[18]

Other students I spoke with had stronger reactions to the negative comments they had overheard. A Christian biology student, when I started to ask a question about how religion comes up around other students, interrupted and quickly responded, "Only when they're making fun of it." He went on to say,

> That's honestly my experience in social settings. It seems like, again, religious individuals tend to be always on the butt of the jokes. Or this is some backwards concept that should be eradicated or removed. I've basically . . . I've sat in and I've overhead people saying, "I don't want any religious freaks joining my lab."[19]

Religious students who hear such negative comments are in a difficult position about how to respond given the small social community of many graduate programs. The Christian psychology student mentioned above, who believed she was the only religious person in her program, described to me how a Mormon church near her department's building would sometimes be the subject of derogatory comments by her peers. These comments made her uncomfortable, but also put her in a difficult position in terms of her relationship with her peers:

With the example with the Mormon Church, most of it I've heard while people are walking out the door, so it almost feels a little bit . . . I don't know the word for it. But it's like when you're the only person who's religious and you're not that religion, do you feel compelled to say, "well, actually I don't think that's a productive comment."

It's almost like being a member of another minority group and you hear someone saying a joke about another minority group. And you say, I don't know anything about their experience, but do I jump in and say "I don't think that's a productive way to speak about it?" And if anything, I do kind of struggle with that sometimes. Do I need to check that?[20]

A few of the religious students I spoke with, who had made their faith known to their peers, recounted feeling more personally attacked by peers. A Christian physics student, for instance, described how a couple of the people he worked with in a lab would engage with him about his faith: "A few times, every week or so, they would get into discussions where they're just kind of talking how dumb religion is and how dumb Christianity is. The one guy that was in my group, he also particularly liked to debate so he could be pretty . . . he could be pretty in my face about it sometimes. It got to the point where I was like, I'm just not even going to talk about this."[21]

Like this student, several other religious students I spoke with felt that at least some of their peers were almost evangelical in advocating for atheism. A female chemistry student who was raised Catholic but now identifies simply as Christian said, "I think when I talked to people in my group about this, it became really clear to me that there are scientists who are atheist who have as much faith in atheism as anyone who is religious has faith in religion."[22] Another chemistry student who identifies as Jewish but does not think of himself as religious similarly told me that, "People who are more militantly atheist will kind of take the discipline and the rationality of science as an automatic reason to say that other people's religion is wrong. This isn't uniform for the atheist population here, but there are people who are hostile about it."[23]

A couple of the religious students I spoke with made an interesting distinction between how those in their graduate program speak about religion in public or groups settings as opposed to more private, inter-personal interactions. In short, these students felt that their peers or even faculty tended to be much more negative or hostile toward religion in public settings and much more respectful or at least neutral in private settings. When I asked a biology student how religion came up in his department, he said,

> Hostile in the open. In private, not so much. My own personal experience is that scientists, at least out in open in public in my experience here, are overwhelmingly hostile to [religion]. That being said, what I have per-sonally found is that in private, when you bring these issues up, they're slightly less hostile than you would sort of assume.[24]

This public–private distinction could reflect an attempt by these students to signal their identity and community allegiance to those around them. That is, in social settings with other scientists, making negative comments about religion might serve to express one's identity and ad-herence to the scientific community. In private, though, this social pres-sure is less of a concern.

Hostility and Disrespect

Overheard comments and direct negative exchanges with peers about religion can, naturally, lead many religious students to feel that there is general hostility and disrespect toward their faith. This student, along with other religious students I spoke with, felt that the assumption of atheism in science was not passive in nature, but rather part of an active hostility toward religion. My survey asked students whether they agreed or disagreed with the following statement: "In general, I feel that peo-ple in my discipline have a negative attitude toward religion." As Table 3.1 shows, 44 percent of students agreed overall with this statement.

TABLE 3.1 Percentage of Science Graduate Students Who Agree that People in Their Disciplines Have Negative Attitudes toward Religion, Overall and by Religiosity

	"In general, I feel that people in my discipline have a negative attitude toward religion."				
By Religiosity	Very religious	Moderately religious	Slightly religious	Not a religious person	Overall
Agree	69%[a]	63%[a]	43%	37%	44%

a. Significantly different from the "not a religious person" percentage at $p<.05$.

However, students who described themselves as very or moderately religious were significantly more likely to say that people in their disciplines have negative attitudes toward religion. Sixty-nine percent of very religious students and 63 percent of moderately religious students agreed with this statement. It is also noteworthy that a sizeable portion of nonreligious students—37 percent—also agreed that people in their disciplines are hostile toward religion.

I also asked students on the survey, "Thinking specifically about your experiences as a graduate student, how often do you feel like you are treated with less respect because of your religion? If you do not identify with a religion, how often does this happen to you because you do not identify with a religion?" The last part of this question was important because, while nonreligious individual may be the numerical and cultural majority in science, there is sizable research showing that in many other contexts nonreligious people, particularly atheists, face hostility and disrespect because they are in the minority.[25] The nonreligious, however, may not see a question about being treated with less respect due to religion as applicable to them, which makes it difficult to know whether a response of "never" is because they do not experience any disrespect due to being nonreligious or because they do not think the question is asking about those experiences. This question thus asks students directly whether they are treated with less respect for not identifying with a religion.

As Table 3.2 shows, 80 percent of science graduate students say they are never treated with less respect because of either their religion or their lack of religion. This means, in turn, that 20 percent of science graduate students feel that such treatment occurs at least occasionally. Nonreligious students are less likely to report such treatment, as only 10 percent say this ever happens, and most of those students report its frequency of occurrence as less than once a year.

As we look at the categories representing more religious students, we see that experiences of being treated with less respect due to religion (or the lack thereof) become more common. Nineteen percent of slightly religious students report any such negative treatment, but this jumps to 46 percent among moderately religious students and to 64 percent among very religious students. We also see that the frequency of being disrespected due to religion (or the lack thereof) increases for more religious students. For instance, only 8 percent of slightly religious students say they are treated with less respect due to religion a few times a year or more. This increases to 24 percent of moderately religious students and

TABLE 3.2 Percentage of Students Who Say They Have Been Treated with Less Respect Because of Their Religion, by Religiosity

	Thinking specifically about your experiences as a graduate student, how often do you feel like you are treated with less respect because of your religion? If you do not identify with a religion, how often does this happen to you because you do not identify with a religion?				
By Religiosity	Very religious	Moderately religious	Slightly religious	Not a religious person	Overall
Never	36%	54%	81%	90%	79%
Less than once a year	11%	22%	11%	7%	10%
A few times a year	32%	19%	7%	3%	8%
A few times a month	11%	4%	1%	0%	2%
At least once a week or more	10%	1%	0%	0%	1%
Total	100%	100%	100%	100%	100%

53 percent of very religious students. As a comparison, 22 percent of the women in my survey report feeling disrespected because of their gender with the same frequency, and 32 percent of the black students report in the survey report feeling disrespected because of their race with the same frequency.[26] For more religious students, then, feeling disrespected because of their religion is a fairly common experience.

Conceal or Reveal?

Feeling that one's religious identity or beliefs are disrespected by other students or faculty does not require those individuals to be aware of that identity or those beliefs. As we have seen, the climate of assumed atheism often leads individuals in science graduate programs to make negative comments in front of a religious student, as it is believed that everyone shares the same views. As we have also seen, there is no guarantee that those negative comments will stop even if other people do know that a student is religious. In fact, a couple of students I spoke with felt that they became a target of those comments, or at least became the perceived spokesperson for religious matters, if others knew of their faith. Yet challenging the assumption of universal atheism in graduate programs would seem to benefit from religious individuals being open about their own faith.[27] This raises a dilemma for religious students: should they make their religious identity known, or should they keep it concealed?

In her study of religion among academic science faculty, Elaine Howard Ecklund noted that "religious scientists generally tried to keep their faith to themselves because of the perception that other faculty in their departments think poorly of religious people and religious ideas." Ecklund argued that this "perpetuates a *closeted faith* and a strong culture of suppression" for religious scientists.[28]

I asked graduate students on my survey whether they agreed or disagreed with the statement, "I conceal or camouflage signs of my religious views or identity around people in my program." As seen in Table 3.3, about 40 percent of very and moderately religious students

TABLE 3.3 Percentage of Science Graduate Students Who Agree that They Conceal Their Religious Identity, by Religiosity

| | "I conceal or camouflage signs of my religious views or identity around people in my graduate program." | | | | |
By Religiosity	Very religious	Moderately religious	Slightly religious	Not a religious person	Overall
Agree	40%[a]	39%[a]	23%[a]	7%	16%

a. Significantly different from the "not a religious person" percentage at $p<.05$.

agreed with this statement, while 23 percent of slightly religious and 7 percent of nonreligious students agreed that they hide their religious views or identity.

In my conversations with them, religious graduate students described their thinking about concealing or revealing their faith to others in their programs. Several students related that they were hesitant to reveal their religious lives, lest they be labeled or judged negatively by peers or faculty. A biology student, for example, made it very clear that he had not and would not reveal his faith to anyone in his program or even in his broader disciplinary community.

> I do not speak of my personal religion. I don't think anybody at work knows that I'm religious. There are some significant repercussions in my field if you are religious. Socially speaking, you will take a very significant hit to your social impression. There are certain enforceable stereotypes about people that hold religious beliefs.[29]

A sociology student described similar reasons for concealing her religious life from others in her program. "I keep it very [concealed] . . . especially in my grad program, I haven't really talked about it. Mostly out of I think more of a personal fear of being not judged but just like I think there can be a lot of negative stereotypes about people being super religious." The student expressed ambivalence about concealing her faith.

I feel a little guilty at times. Especially spiritually, that I can't share that, or I feel like I should be able to share that with other people. I think at times it would be nice to be able to talk to people about that. Yeah, there's definitely times when I'm like, "Oh I wish I could talk about this." Or I feel like I'm not being a good Christian because I'm not open about it.[30]

Indeed, although many individuals with stigmatized identities think that concealing those identities will help them connect with the larger group, research has found that this concealment itself often ends up being harmful to their own psychological well-being and to their sense of connection to others.[31]

Of course, some students might conceal their religiosity for part of their time in graduate school and then open up about it later. A sociology student, different from the one above, took what she saw as a strategic route in concealing her religious faith at first but eventually revealing it to her peers:

I did not tell anyone in my cohort [that I am religious] for three years, because the assumptions that go with that are: you don't think critically, you don't believe in science, right? I wanted them to know me on my merits for what I could bring to the table as a scholar, and then have this be something that's introduced later and maybe change their opinions. But it wouldn't skew their idea of who I am from the get-go, and then make it harder for me to dig myself out of that hole.[32]

A couple of students I spoke with who had made connections to other religious graduate students, whether in their department or elsewhere on campus, took steps to hide the nature of these relationships. For instance, the Christian biology student quoted earlier, who spoke of the "significant repercussions" of being religious in his program, had made connections to a few other actively practicing Christian, Jewish, and Muslim students through what he called "circumstance and happenstance." He told me that "the joke is, we are like Hydra from the

Avengers, where we kind of contact each other almost in an underground setting because we don't want to be seen to be discussing religion
openly for fear of either offending people or have other people judge us
based on our opinions."[33]

A Jewish chemistry student, who did not consider himself particularly religious, was aware of a similar underground group of religious
individuals in his program.

> There's a group within my lab that will get together for a prayer circle
> daily. They don't actually mention this to any of the other people in the
> group. Or at least, they don't usually tell people directly if they're doing
> something like this, but instead will try to, sort of say, "We need the room
> to discuss our research." I think that they feel stigma about their religious
> beliefs from the scientific community broadly.[34]

At the end of his description of these covert religious meetings, this
student explicitly stated what all of these students implicitly struggle
with: the perceived stigma associated with being a religious individual
in science. That is, there is a fear that being known as religious almost
instantly taints and discredits a student in the social community both
within their graduate programs and the broader scientific community.

Awkward Interactions

The sociologist Erving Goffman, who wrote the foundational work on
social stigma, noted that interactions between those who are stigmatized
and those who are not stigmatized ("normals") are often defined by their
awkwardness.[35] Stigmatized individuals are often on edge around normal individuals because they worry about how they are being perceived.
This can lead the stigmatized to resort to "defensive cowering," "hostile
bravado," or rotating between the two reactions. "Normal" individuals,
for their part, are not comfortable either, when interacting with stigmatized individuals, as they often alternate between showing a type of

morbid curiosity in the stigmatized individual and being concerned that they are showing too much awareness of the stigma.

Some of the religious students who did reveal their religiosity to those in their program described such exchanges. A physics student explained the awkwardness of his mealtime prayers:

> I tend to pray before I eat. And that's a really weird thing if I go to conferences, or places where I might want to apply here [for a job] and the people that I'm sitting with or eating with are looking at me. Are they not going to want to hire me if I pray before I eat? It's weird.[36]

Similarly, a chemistry student who told me she is "very open" about her religiosity described how some people in her program react:

> It definitely can get uncomfortable at times. Some of my coworkers are much more open to it and much more like, "oh, okay, that's like your thing, and that's cool." And other people, you can tell they get uncomfortable, and they change the subject, and then that makes me uncomfortable, just because they're uncomfortable. They're just real awkward about it. It's not something that's deterred me in any way from being who I am, but I hate the awkward interactions because it just seems unnecessary. Like, if someone tells me they're into mountain biking, I'm not like, "oh, you like to mountain bike, that's weird." I don't know, to me it's not really something that needs to be awkward, but it can be.[37]

Stereotypes and Internalized Doubts

Groups that are underrepresented in science are often subject to (incorrect) stereotypes about their scientific abilities.[38] These stereotypes then become a supposed explanation for their underrepresentation in science. While members of these groups naturally reject them, the prevalence of such stereotypes can nonetheless become internalized by the very individuals they target. That is, minority individuals' awareness of these stereotypes can produce doubts and anxieties that, ironically, harm their performance in science. As an analogy, you might walk in a perfectly normal fashion, but if people start telling you that your gait is strange then you might start to subtly doubt and over-think it, which ultimately throws off how you walk. This dynamic has been studied extensively in the context of gender and racial minorities in science.[39]

One study has looked at this "stereotype threat" concept in the con-text of religion and science. The social psychologist Kimberly Rios and colleagues conducted several experiments that showed no difference in performance on science-related tasks between Christians and non-Christians *unless* Christians were first exposed to statements express-ing a stereotype that Christians were less capable in science. When first exposed to such stereotypes, Christians actually performed worse on science-related tasks. In other words, the internalized doubts and anxi-eties about being part of the stereotyped group actually harmed the in-dividuals' performance.[40]

We have already seen that religious students in science are highly aware of stereotypes concerning their supposed diminished abilities in science, but other religious students also mentioned awareness of such stereotypes. A biology student, for instance, told me,

> Sometimes I'll mention something about a church event, and people will act surprised that someone is religious, and I don't know if that's good or bad. And I don't really want to find out if it's a good or bad surprise. People in my program have made comments online about how they don't think people who have religious views could ever be a good scientist just because that's illogical and science is about logic.[41]

Similarly, when explaining to me her hesitancy to be more open about her religious identity, a psychology student explained, "I think it would influence their view of me as a scientist."

This question of whether being religious makes an individual a less capable scientist was implicit or explicit in many of the conservations I had with religious students. Of course, these students naturally rejected these concerns. However, the very presence of this question and the need to have a conversation about it is notable. Given studies like Rios's, we must wonder how often these students' performance in their graduate programs is affected by these stereotypes.

Issues of Accommodation

While issues concerning stereotypes and interpersonal disrespect were some of the most common adverse experiences religious students described to me, a handful also reported experiences with more organizational forms of hostility toward their faith. Some of these involved a lack of awareness or willingness by their graduate programs to accommodate religious practices or beliefs. A chemistry student described one such incident involving a conflict between Sunday worship and a departmental event:

> The department wanted to have a retreat on the weekend to talk about science issues, but they wanted to have it on a Saturday night into Sunday. There were several of us who were concerned about this because it was on a Sunday, and we were having to decide between going to a church, and doing our religious obligations versus this quasi-required department retreat. Initially, it was blown off as, like, I don't know why this is such a problem for you all . . . it's just one weekend. Eventually, we were able to just say that we will only come for Saturday.[42]

Other examples that came up in my conversations involve religiously derived dietary restrictions. A Muslim chemistry student, for instance, told me that her department "had a big banquet . . . it was a big, five-course, black tie thing. They cooked two of the five courses in alcohol." Following the strictures of her faith, she did not consume alcohol, so when submitting her RSVP she requested that her food be cooked "on the side" without alcohol. This, she said, "caused this huge, big thing in the department. The person in charge of it got mad and then tried to pretend that they hadn't told me no."[43] Naturally, issues like these led many of these students to feel that their programs see their beliefs and practices, at best, as an inconvenience or, at worst, entirely unwelcome.

From Climate to Relationships

A grad student's relationships with those around them in their program can have a significant influence on their well-being and even their success. Given the data and stories we have engaged with, one might assume that many religious students find it impossible to form positive relationships with peers and faculty. As the next chapter reveals, however, the reality is often more nuanced.

4

Advisors and Peers

Catherine

When I talked with Catherine, she was just about to graduate with her PhD in psychology. She had already acquired a tenure-track faculty position, so she was justifiably excited about starting the next stage of her career. This might have contributed to her being particularly open and reflective about her graduate school experiences. On the whole, Catherine viewed her experiences as overwhelmingly positive. This included her experiences in classes and with the faculty in her program:

> The faculty were so supportive. I mean they've just really. . . . I told them that the last six years have been the best of my life. And that's absolutely unequivocally true. Their support and teaching and challenging and asking the critical and tough questions have been a big part of that.[1]

Catherine also pointed to her relationships with other students in her program as strongly contributing to her positive grad school experience:

> So, in our cohort, we had four students who started the program together. And we were very close the first year because we took all of the same classes and had the exact same schedule. I think we could have stood to be maybe less close. I think we were like, "Oh my God, if I have to see people [anymore]." I mean, it built a very close-knit community. So in that way it was good. Yeah, I really, I think I have genuine friendships with not only my cohort, maybe really close with my cohort, but with other students in the psychology program.

Catherine did note that while she considers her peers in her program "very close friends," she did not necessarily socialize with them much outside of work because of her own family life. As she explains, "I'm a mom of two and I have a really busy partner, I don't have time to really cultivate those relationships."

Of all the relationships that appear to have bolstered Catherine's experience in grad school, her relationship with her advisor was clearly the most important. She described the start of this relationship to me:

> So I had applied, and I wound up getting shortlisted. I heard from my to-be-advisor and she had two students ahead of me on her shortlist. And the stars really aligned and one of the students ahead of me said no. I said yes, and [my advisor] called me. I think I met with her once before this and we had an amazing meeting. And so she called me and she's like, "You want to work with me," and I did the thing you're never supposed to do which is say yes right away. I was like, "Yes. I'm in."
>
> And that just really, that was the beginning of our relationship and . . . We have been so productive and we've just, we've exceeded my wildest dreams in terms of what we've accomplished together, what I've been able to do in the constructs of this program. So in terms of the dimensions of the relationship, I mean it is personal, it is professional. She mentors the whole person.

Although it is possible that her relationship with her advisor would have been positive regardless, Catherine pointed to their shared faith as a major factor in their dynamic. Catherine described herself as a "devout Catholic, cradle Catholic." She saw her faith as a central part of her biography, her relationships, and her approach to her scientific work:

> My grandparents were Catholic, and so we would do church and then we would have our brunches, and it was just this really warm family environment. The priest who baptized me was a close friend of our family for fifteen years. [Catholicism] was a huge part of how I grew up.

Catherine did not know that her advisor was also a practicing Catholic when she applied to or accepted her position in the graduate program. "Yeah, it was a surprise. I didn't know any of this about her [religion]. It was so serendipitous." Although she could not be sure of what her experience would have been like if her advisor was not Catholic, she did believe that it benefitted her:

> I definitely felt more supported, because I felt like I could bring my whole self to her. I talked to her across all sorts of domains, and if I had had an advisor that was judgmental [about religion] in the way that some of the other people I know are, that would have felt like a taboo topic, and that would have been very difficult. I may have not felt like I could hack it in a secular world if I had an advisor like that. It might have made the pendulum swing further, whereas I think sometimes we need people who have a strong religious identity in secular world, because otherwise we just have these two non-overlapping systems that, I don't know, seem sort of silly to preach to the choir all the time, like influence the people who maybe haven't been exposed to the work.

Grad school can at times be intensely intimate, as students are often working and studying very closely with each other and their faculty mentors. Somewhat paradoxically, grad school can also be extremely socially isolating at times, as students focus on their dissertation and other research projects alone for long periods of time. How students navigate relationships with peers and faculty can play a significant role in their experience and success in grad school. Students who clash with their peers or who do not have a positive relationship with their faculty advisors often struggle during those periods of intense closeness *and* during those periods of isolation. During the former, those poor relationships often lead to stress and anxiety. During the latter, those poor relationships mean that that student lacks a support system to buffer potential feelings of isolation.

We have already seen how religion can at times be a source of stigma and conflict for religious students. That is not, however, the only way religion can play a role in religious students' relationships in grad school.

Choosing an Advisor

Individuals applying to graduate programs will often receive advice about what they should consider when deciding where to apply and ultimately where to go. Some advice-givers will naturally point to the prestige of the specific graduate program or the university. Is it a nationally ranked program? Is its ranking rising or falling? Others will point to the financial support being offered by programs. How much is the stipend? How many years of support are guaranteed? Will you be earning your stipend as a teaching assistant or research assistant, or will you be on a fellowship?

Questions of prestige and financial support likely seem natural even to those unfamiliar with exactly how graduate school works, as they are similar to the questions that many would ask about deciding where to go for one's undergraduate degree. Those without much familiarity with graduate school, or with science PhD programs in particular, may not appreciate the importance of asking questions about the student's potential faculty mentor or advisor.

Most science PhD programs take the form of an apprenticeship. Students are often accepted into the program with the intention that they will be working under the supervision of a particular faculty member. It is not always easy to change advisors once one begins a program, since doing so would mean changing research areas and other faculty may not want to work with a student that they did not accept in the first place. Because of this, the advisor has a significant amount of control and power over the student's experiences in the program.

Ideally, an advisor actively provides opportunities and training that benefit the student's growth as a scientist while also providing social and psychological support. As Catherine put it above, an ideal advisor will mentor "the whole person." In less-than-ideal situations, advisors may be aloof or disinterested in their mentees, or they might see their students simply as workhorses for their own careers and show little concern for their students' growth as professional scientists. In worst-case scenarios, advisors can be outright abusive toward their students.

My interviews with students illustrated the full range of these experiences, from extremely positive . . .

She's incredibly supportive, I would say. Whenever things go poorly in the lab, I think she's more looking it as not something wrong with me and is very recognizing of the fact that things just do go wrong, and it's okay, and we can try again. She just kept helping me troubleshoot and was never angry or upset with me.[2]

. . . to nice but hands-off . . .

When I was just starting out, I wasn't really given a project . . . I was just told, "Find something to work on," you know? And that was really, really challenging. Like we do have individual, one-on-one meetings every six weeks or so. But in terms of being invested in project directions and help with deciding where to publish and that kind of stuff, he very much leaves that up to us.[3]

. . . to distant and demanding . . .

He's really enthusiastic, but also very demanding. So he expects you to work pretty hard and late hours. So, I'd say it's, I guess, as cordial. I wouldn't say friendly because, he's, he only shows up in lab every once in a while.[4]

. . . to outright negative:

She's pushes us a lot and wants us to get a lot done. We haven't really gotten the results I think she was hoping for it. I don't know. It was better in the beginning. Now I have a lot of negative feelings toward her. I think when she's stressed out, she'll kind of lash out at us, say some mean, nasty things. I think about switching [advisors] all the time.[5]

Beyond affecting their experience in grad school itself, an advisor can have a major influence on a student's career trajectory, especially if the student desires to obtain a job as an academic scientist. Search committees often weigh heavily who the student worked with in grad school and that advisor's recommendation letter. Advisors can also help favored students' careers by utilizing their professional networks and relationships to lobby for them.[6]

Given all of this, questions about a potential faculty advisor should be at the forefront of every potential grad student's mind when choosing a program. Is there someone at this program who conducts research that they want to be a part of? Is this person prominent in their field? Does that person have a successful record of mentoring students and placing them in the types of careers that you are interested in pursuing? What do their past or current students have to say about that faculty member?

Such considerations likely seem intuitive, but what about things like a potential advisor's race, gender, or religion? Do such demographic characteristics play a role in a student's choice of an advisor?

Demographic Matching

Obtaining a PhD in the sciences is difficult enough, but students who are part of groups that are typically underrepresented in the sciences, such as women and some racial or ethnic minorities, face a number of additional challenges to successfully navigating the process. These students often face stereotypes about their scientific commitment or abilities. Studies have shown, for instance, that faculty in the sciences tend to be more critical toward and less invested in female students even if they have they have the exact same background and accomplishments of a male peer. Interestingly, this bias is found among female faculty as well.[7]

Even if such biases, discrimination, and even harassment did not exist, students from underrepresented groups still must face the daily reality that few or none of their peers and faculty look like them or truly understand their background and perspectives. That is, there is always an awareness of being different, and a feeling of social isolation.

Although obviously not a panacea, some have suggested that students from underrepresented groups would benefit from working with an advisor who matches their underrepresented demographic characteristic(s). That is, women in science would benefit from having a woman as an advisor, Black students would benefit from having a Black advisor, and so on.[8]

Research on whether students actually benefit from having a demographically matched advisor has produced mixed conclusions. Some studies have found that students who demographically match their advisors benefit in terms of the degree to which they feel psychologically and socially supported by their advisor. Those same studies, though, have found that these students do not appear to benefit in terms of their academic outcomes. Similarly, some studies have found that the career outcomes of science students who demographically matched their advisors are better than those who did not match their advisors, while others have found no such career benefits.[9]

These mixed findings might in part be a function of different methods and disciplines being considered, but they might also be a function of demographic matching being a "poor proxy for other, more meaningful types of matches" between students and advisors.[10] One study of science students found that once one accounts for students' perceptions that their advisors share similar personalities and values that are similar to themselves, the fact of being demographically matched has no additional benefit.[11] In other words, demographic matching *might* serve as a rough guess that a student and advisor will share the same values and personality (or at least think that they do). But sharing values and personality can be obtained outside of a demographically matched student and advisor; being matched, in and of itself, does not seem to have an intrinsic benefit.

In any case, almost all of the discussion about the benefits of demographic matching between grad students and advisors has focused on gender and race matching. No one has considered religion as a relevant characteristic. If, however, demographic matching is really about matching values, then religion would seem to be an important part of the conversation, whether a student identifies as an atheist or as religious.

On my survey, I asked students how important it is to them for their advisor to match their gender, race, and religion. Table 4.1 shows that the majority of students said that matching their advisor's gender, race, and religion is not important. Of the three, gender matching is the most likely to be rated at least a little important, with about one in five students saying it is very, somewhat, or a little important. Religion is the least likely to be rated at least a little important.

Of course, these overall percentages are probably not the numbers we should focus on. We would expect, for several reasons, that individuals who are part of groups representing numerical or cultural minorities in science would be more likely to rate demographic matching as important.[12] We might expect, for instance, that female students might place more importance on gender matching than male students would, given that female students tend to be in the numerical and sociocultural

TABLE 4.1 Importance Graduate Students Place on Matching Advisor's Demographic Characteristics, by Type of Characteristic

	How important is it that your primary faculty advisor is of the same . . .		
	. . . race or ethnicity as you?	. . . gender as you?	. . . religion as you?
Very important to me	2.1%	3.5%	0.2%
Somewhat important to me	3.1%	5.7%	1.1%
A little important to me	6.9%	11.1%	3.6%
Not important to me	87.9%	79.7%	95.1%
Total	100%	100%	100%

minority in science. This is what the data show for the gender and race questions. Almost all male students (94.3%) say that matching their advisor's gender is not important to them at all. A little over a third of female students (37.6%), though, place at least a little importance on matching their advisor's gender, and 7.6 percent say that this matching is very important to them. We find similar patterns when looking at the race-matching question. Almost all White students (94.1%) say that matching their advisor's race is not important to them at all. Over two-thirds of Black students (68.9%), though, say that matching their advisor's race is at least a little important to them, and 24.2 percent rate this as very important to them.

Surprisingly, though, we do not find the same pattern when looking at the religion-matching question. Students who identify as atheist look almost identical to those who identify as Christian. Specifically, 92.9 percent of atheist students and 92.2 percent of Christian students say that their advisor's religion is not important to them at all.[13] Even if we look at self-rated religiosity, we find that 85.6 percent of very religious students say that their advisor's religion is not important to them at all.

Why is an advisor's religion rated as unimportant, even by students who identify with a particular religion, or as generally religious? Saying that this characteristic is irrelevant to the student–advisor relationship seems unsatisfactory and unpersuasive, especially if demographic matching is really a proxy for finding someone who shares particular values. There is no obvious reason to think that being able to share one's religious faith or, for that matter, one's lack of faith, with one's advisor would not provide the same social and psychological benefits that sharing one's experiences as a woman or racial minority in science would provide.

There is a clear difference in the nature of religious identities relative to gender and racial identities. A person's religion is often a more invisible, and therefore concealable, characteristic than gender or race. Given this, it is possible that students simply think that they cannot consider it because it would be impolite to inquire about a potential advisor's religion. But this is not an entirely satisfactory explanation for why religious students would rate their advisor's religion as unimportant. After all, a student can believe that sharing their advisor's religion is important while also thinking that they probably cannot ask about it nor do much about it if they do not share a religion.

The more likely explanation for why an advisor's religion is rated unimportant, even by religious students, is that religion is simply not part of the conversation when it comes to the factors that students should consider when choosing advisors. This, of course, is a function of the larger culture of professional science that sees religion as irrelevant at best, and contradictory at worst, to the pursuit of science. As a result, even students who identify with a religion and take their faith quite seriously do not even think that considering their advisor's religion is something that they could or should do. They may also assume, given this professional culture of assumed atheism, that their advisor will obviously not be religious. Moreover, looking for an advisor who shares a student's religion will require the student to reveal their own religiosity. Given the stigma involved with being religious in the scientific community, religious students may simply be resigned to accepting that their advisor's religion is not or cannot be important to them.

When Religion Comes Up

Although one's religious identity and religious life can be concealed to some extent, it can become difficult to keep it entirely hidden when a student works closely with an advisor for five or more years. Many of the religious students I spoke with said that at one point or another their religion did come up. This often seemed to happen under fairly mundane circumstances. A Mormon student, for instance, noted that one day she wore a Brigham Young University to the office. "My advisor asked, 'Oh, did you go there? Are you LDS (Latter-day Saint)?' And I said, 'Yes.' And he was like, 'Oh, cool. I had a friend [who was Mormon] . . .' So, it was brought up that way, but hasn't been mentioned since or before."[14] Several students mentioned that discussions surrounding holidays often prompt some revelation of individuals' religious faiths. I asked a student whether religion ever comes up with her advisor. "Not a ton," she said.

> Just that he's Jewish. I'm a Christian. We'll wish each other whatever happy holiday it is. Usually around when the holidays are coming up for scheduling or meeting or something we'll be mindful of that. We might talk about like, "Oh, what do you do at Passover? What do you do at Easter? How was your Hanukkah? How was your Christmas?" Those kinds of discussions. But never really an in-depth discussion about what it means to him to be Jewish, what it means to me to be Christian or anything like that.[15]

As can be seen in both of these students' quotations, while religion does eventually come up as students develop relationships with their advisors, it tends to stay somewhat superficial.

One student, who identified as Hindu, felt that her advisor was more "reticent" to discuss the student's religious identity relative to other parts of her identity. Yet this student made it clear to me that her religious life was not a secret from her advisor. "I think she knows [I'm Hindu]. She knows. And I can say I'm going home for a religious holiday or, 'This is what I practice,' or, 'This is what I do.'"[16]

We should not discount the importance of even these somewhat superficial acknowledgements of a student's religious life. Indeed, a couple of students explained that simply being able to be open about their religious identity in front of their advisor is important to them, even if it does not lead to in-depth conversations. A biology student told me,

> [My advisor] is the one person who I have spoken to about religion and has been not attacking. So I know that we probably don't have the same views but just knowing that there's at least one professor out there that doesn't think that I'm not welcome in science sort of makes me like I'm worthy of being a scientist here. That's great that we've had those conversations.[17]

Another student, also in a biology program, expressed a similar appreciation for his advisor's openness to religion:

> My advisor is surprisingly not hostile to religion. I'm pretty sure he's not religious, or I think he has said that, "I don't believe in gods or whatever." At the same time, my advisor is not a religiously hostile person. That is what I think is very interesting about him. And for that I respect him quite a bit. Because some of my other professors throughout campus that I have sort of seen or heard are definitely what I would describe as being overtly hostile.[18]

Although rare, a couple of the religious students I spoke with actually made more meaningful and in-depth connections to their advisor through their faith. Like Catherine, whom we met at the start of this chapter, another psychology student found that her advisor shared her Christianity, and this played an active role in their relationship:

> He identifies as a Christian himself, so I'll share scriptures with him and have prayed with him before. He's prayed with me before at presentations and conferences. I think [our shared religion] enhanced our relationship. I also knew we share the same things before I came because a previous student mentioned to me that like they had prayed together at times and that was very attractive for me as a student. You have the same or similar background, so yeah I think it enhanced it. But I also think our relationship would still be okay if that wasn't there; it's just a bonus for me.[19]

Similarly, a sociology student described to me how his advisor's own exploration of his spirituality has positively influenced their relationship:

> My advisor has gotten increasingly interested in his own forms of spirituality over the past few years, and I feel like I have felt more connection

to that than I would have otherwise because I've also been developing my spiritual practice over those years. So I've felt more camaraderie than I think I otherwise would have in that.[20]

Religion as Student-Advisor Relationship Strain?

Given the feelings of hostility and stigma toward their faith that many religious students feel in their graduate programs, or in the scientific community in general, we might expect that religious students would report poorer relationships with their advisor when compared to non-religious students. That is, it would be natural to think that advisors may treat religious students poorly or at least differently from nonreligious students. Or, at the very least, we might expect that religious students' internalized feelings of stigma and isolation might harm their ability to connect with their advisor.

My survey data, however, finds little evidence that students' religiosity is a point of conflict or strain on students' relationships with their advisors. I asked all students their level of agreement with the statement, "My advisor conveys feelings of respect for me as an individual." The data do not show any notable differences in student responses based on the student's religiosity. Just over half (51.8%) of very religious students strongly agree that their advisor conveys feelings of respect for them, as compared to 50.1 percent of moderately religious students, 52.0 percent of slightly religious students, and 47.6 percent of nonreligious students. I also asked students their level of agreement with the statement, "My advisor encourages me to prepare for advancement in this program." Again, there are no statistically significant differences across levels of student religiosity. Just over half (51.9%) of very religious students strongly agree with this statement, as compared to 46.3 percent of moderately religious, 48.8 percent of slightly religious, and 46.2 percent of nonreligious students.

How do we reconcile the stigma and hostility felt by many religious students in their science programs—including coming from faculty at times—with the relatively positive, or at least neutral, role of religion in religious students' relationships with their advisors? One possibility is that religious students, whether intentionally or not, have selected advisors who are religious themselves or at least not hostile toward religion and religious students. While such sorting likely does occur, it is also possible that the public side of "religion and science" in these programs is much different from the private side. The public side is one in which students, and to some extent faculty, establish and negotiate their image as scientists. Speaking negatively about religion may be seen as a way to establish an image as a "real scientist." But as individuals form personal relationships and interact as colleagues or as mentors and mentees, there is less motivation to put on a public show. It is also difficult to maintain crude stereotypes of the people sitting across the desk from you as they challenge the very assumptions of those stereotypes.

Advisors are not the only relationships that are important to students' experiences in grad school, nor are they the only ones important for students' development as scientists. Graduate students' peers not only serve as sources of friendship and support, but can also represent research collaborators. How does religion factor into these potential relationships?

Cohorts, Peers, and Community

The importance and intensity of the advisor-student relationship is a unique feature of the grad school experience, at least relative to what most students experience as undergraduates. Students' relationships with other students, though, also take on a different dynamic in grad school than what they might have experienced as an undergraduate. As undergraduates, students move across campus taking classes containing dozens or even hundreds of other students. When class is over, they move to another class or go back to their dorms or apartments. While undergraduates might start recognizing some familiar faces, students in any particular class often begin and end the semester as strangers.

PhD programs, on the other hand, only accept a handful of students each year. Smaller programs may only have four or five new students a

year, while larger programs may accept fifteen to twenty students. Regardless, those newly accepted students will usually take all of the same
classes as a group for at least the first year, and sometimes multiple
years. This "cohort" will frequently share office and lab space, many
times in the same building where they are taking those classes. In short,
whether a student likes it or not, they will be seeing *a lot* of the other
students in their grad program, especially those students who began the
program with them. Not surprisingly, the relationships between students can have a significant impact on individual students' experiences
and the group as a whole.[21] This was reflected in my conversations with
students.

A psychology student described how she was one of five students who
began her program together:

> I think we got very close, very fast at the beginning of the program for a
> number of different positive and negative circumstances. And it was like,
> "We're all in this together." So, we've had to support each other. It was very
> quickly like, "Oh! These people are going to be my family. These people
> are going to be the people who I'm going to rely on for the next five years,
> at least." So, I think there was that expectation that we were going to get
> together and make fast friends really quickly. And we have. And I rely on
> them for things in the program.[22]

Other students I spoke with did not have the same positive experience
and feelings for their cohort. A biology student, for instance, explained
how conflict within his student group ruined their group's bonding:

> My cohort basically experienced the equivalent of a Game of Thrones-
> type split where two persons with major attitudes and major personality
> intentionally sabotaged each other. This particular event destroyed any
> cohesion that my year has to the point where I think I and maybe one
> other student can talk to everybody on both sides, but people in my year,
> they just don't talk to each other.

This is one of these very interesting experiences. A lot of people will be able to look back at their graduate-school days and say that some of the friends that I've made here are the best that I'll have in my life. In my case, I think I can count for maybe one or two. My cohort was basically absolutely destroyed by essentially a year and a half worth of drama by two very polarizing figures.

Students can face challenges in forming positive relationships with their cohort and other students in their departments for a number of reasons. But how might religion present a challenge to these relationships? We have already seen that direct or indirect negative comments about a student's religiosity can be one obvious obstacle toward forming positive relationships with peers. But this is not the only way a student's religiosity might play a part.

Religion, Alcohol, and Bonding

The prominent role of alcohol in the college life is well known. Indeed, television and movie portrayals of college life often center around or at least feature heavy alcohol consumption.[23] While student drinking can be associated with positive experiences, it also tends to come with many negative consequences.[24] Despite those repercussions, many college students see heavy alcohol consumption as a central part of the college experience.[25]

Most of the conversation and research on alcohol in college life focuses on undergraduates, which makes sense given that undergraduates are the largest part of the student population and the group that most people associate with college. But alcohol also has a prominent role in the grad school experience as well, even if that role is of a typically different nature than among undergraduates.[26]

While grad students can and do throw the type of alcohol-heavy "ragers" that we might think of when imagining college parties, drinking in grad school is often more muted and not motivated simply by the desire to drink.[27] Rather, it might consist of a cohort of first-year students going every week to have a drink after a particularly challenging class to debrief and de-stress. Or it might be a few students discussing a research project at a bar with their advisor. Or, when hosting a prominent guest speaker, a department might host a reception where beer and wine is served. Moreover, scientific conferences often feature happy hours that are part social gatherings and part professional networking events. In short, alcohol is often in the background of a grad student's professional development.

For individuals who do not drink alcohol, the organization of social and professional activities around bars, happy hours, and receptions featuring alcohol can be awkward to navigate. While an individual obviously does not have to be religious to have a reason to abstain from alcohol, religiosity is one salient motivation. Research shows, in fact, that religiosity is associated with less alcohol consumption among college students and the population in general.[28]

The issue of alcohol consumption came up in several of the conversations I had with graduate students. In some cases, a student mentioned that they were aware of other students' religiosity mainly because those students did not drink or join activities at bars. In other cases, students mentioned how their religiosity affected their relationships in grad school.[29] When I asked a Christian chemistry student, for instance, whether his religious identity or beliefs influenced he relationship with other students, he told me, "Well, I think probably one of the biggest things is because of my religious identity I don't drink alcohol, and there's a lot of alcohol in grad school. So yeah, so I think that separates me a little bit from some of the other students."[30]

When I asked a Muslim physics student the same question he told me,

Yeah, because I don't drink for example, and most of the gatherings they have drinks . . . that's why I sometimes avoid those gatherings. It definitely affected my relationships. I would say that if I wasn't religious or practicing or anything, it would've made me more involved and more engaged in the department.[31]

A different Christian chemistry student had similar thoughts, telling me,

I don't drink alcohol or smoke tobacco or do some certain things that would harm our bodies. That definitely affects social interactions some-times. I think grad students in general and particular chemists, a lot of their social activities involve drinking. Or sometimes are exclusively just drinking. So that definitely impacts [my relationships]. Occasionally it's been maybe a reason why I haven't become closer with some people.[32]

While a faith-based prohibition against consuming alcohol might present one barrier to forming strong relationships with peers, it is not the only barrier that a student's religion might present. Another barrier is simply the fact that one's faith often presents a separate set of demands for one's time and energy.

A Broader Community

Religious students who are involved in a congregational or faith commu-nity also attend religious services, participate in prayer or bible studies, play on congregational sports teams, volunteer with co-attendees, and so forth. As a psychology student told me about her church involvement: "It's a huge part of my life, so I'm part of a youth group, and church on Sundays and things like that. And I'm always doing stuff for my church."[33] When I asked a physics student how other students came to know about her religious life, she jokingly told me, "I go to church a lot. So often, it will be at a 'thing' on Saturday night when [I tell other students], 'Okay, I've got to go to bed because I got to get up in the morning.'"[34]

Religious students' involvement in a religious community not only shapes their use of time but also their relationships. Religious students who are active in congregational communities have a social network that goes beyond their lab or even their campus. This expanded so-cial network likely benefits students in many ways, especially if their school-based community is weak or even negative.[35] One biology student explained to me how his church community has served as a support system:

> A positive thing has definitely been that going to church or church activities is a good break for me from school. And yeah, kind of gives me a reason to not be thinking about school and science all the time. Also, I feel like I have kind of an automatic support system that starts before I had my network in the department for support as well.[36]

A chemistry student also described how his church community has helped him through challenges that have occurred during grad school:

> My wife and I are both very active in our church, so we have a very large friend base in the community. We have also just had a couple of personal hardships while in grad school, and that can be really derailing for your life. Having a church that we belong to, that we feel very much a part of the community, and not just the [university] community, but then also a part of this really great church family community has really helped us through some challenging times. It's been something where having a community, having people that I know and trust, even though they don't really understand what I'm going through, I get to see that kind of outside world and realize grad school is not the entirety of life.[37]

Although a student's religion-based social ties may occasionally overlap with their science-based ties, they usually appeared to consist heavily of those outside of the student's department, university, or the larger scientific community. Catherine, whom we met at the beginning of this chapter, said that her closest friends come from her church community, which is "largely separate" from her university colleagues.[38] Comments like these were made by several other religious students. A physics student, for instance, described the diversity of his religion-based social group:

I have a small group. . . . It's like a bible study group. We get together and stuff. There are not a lot of people that do science [in the group]. There are a lot of doctors, people in medicine, then other people doing other things that might not be doing a graduate degree or anything like that.[39]

Asked about her primary social group in grad school, a chemistry student said,

My primary community is more outside of grad school . . . mostly from my church or from a campus [religion] group. I like being able to step out of science and not talk about work all the time. So it's nice to hang out with people that are not in the sciences, because for whatever reason a lot of people in science can't leave work at work. And so even if you, you know, go out to lunch with coworkers or go out to dinner or whatever, it's like, "Oh, my experiments didn't work," or "This is working," or "I need to write this draft." And it's just, it's annoying, sometimes, like, can we just leave the lab in lab and just talk about life?[40]

My survey data finds some evidence that student's religious involvement can have an impact on their social relationships within their graduate programs, at least among the most religious students. For instance, I asked students their level of agreement with the statement, "I spend most of my time outside of classes and the office socializing with people from this program." As seen in Table 4.2, 20 percent of students who say they attend religious services more than once a week and 29 percent of students who attend weekly agree with this statement, as compared to 37 percent of students who say they never attend religious services. I also asked students their level of agreement with the statement, "Being in this discipline is a major factor in my social relationships." Again, 28 percent of students attending religious services more than once a week and 38 percent of students attending weekly agree with statement, as compared to 48 percent of students who never attend religious services.

TABLE 4.2 Strength of Social Ties to Graduate Program, by Frequency of
Religious Service Attendance

Percent Agreeing	More than once a week	Once a week	Once a month	Once or twice a year	Less than once a year	Never	Overall
		Frequency of Religious Service Attendance					
I spend most of my time outside of classes and the office socializing with people from this program.[a]	19.8%	29.3%	34.6%	35.9%	30.9%	37.1%	34.9%
Being in this discipline is a major factor in my social relationships.[b]	28.1%	38.2%	40.4%	42.1%	49.6%	47.8%	45.2%

a. Pearson's correlation = -0.08, $p < .01$ (note: utilizing all five responses for agreement variable)
b. Pearson's correlation = -0.12, $p < .01$ (note: utilizing all five responses for agreement variable)

In short, students who are active in a religious community while in grad school spend more of their time and form more of their relationships outside of their programs. Is this a bad thing? The answer depends on your perspective. On the one hand, there can be many benefits to having a more diverse social network. Different types of social ties can provide different types of support, and sometimes useful information and opportunities can be found by extending one's network beyond a single group.[41] On the other hand, diverse social networks can provide competing messages concerning a student's goals and roles.[42] The goals and roles advocated by a student's religious community, for instance, may not be "on message" with the goals and roles advocated for by their science community. Indeed, studies have found that graduate students who have strong relationships outside of their academic bubbles tend not to buy into their departments' messages that research and research-based academic careers are more important than teaching or other personal and professional activities.[43] The next two chapters explore these issues in more depth.

5

Identity and Purpose

Eric

Eric was getting close to receiving his PhD in physics when I spoke with him. His studies were the culmination of an interest in science that was sparked when he was a teenager:

> I guess the first time that I really thought I'd like to be a physicist is probably in high school. I found that I read a lot of science articles, and I really enjoyed reading certain magazines that were about science. So I found it really enjoyable just learning about science, and the books that I picked up on the subject tended to be on physics.[1]

Eric's religious faith had already been a major part of his life when his interest in physics developed. "I have been a Christian for as long as I can remember. Growing up, going to church. Yeah. Both my parents are Christians." He describes his religiosity as largely "consistent" throughout his life.

Eric's faith and scientific interests became intertwined very early on. He told me that he "was particularly interested in the philosophical and theological implications of what some of the physics predictions were." This led him to read many of the well-known Christian scientists who have spoken and written about their own faith.

> Paul Davies is one who has written books on physics and, kind of like the boundary between physics and faith. And then, John Polkinghorne is another writer who I've been inspired by. I guess another one would be Charles Townes. He's the guy who invented the laser . . . won the Nobel

Prize for the maser. I have been fairly inspired by his work and how much he attributed to his faith in terms of his discoveries. Francis Collins is another fairly influential figure for me. I have heard him speak a few times. He's pretty good.

I asked Eric if many of his friends in high school were reading books on the intersections between physics, philosophy, and theology, to which he dryly responds, "Yeah . . . I guess that was unusual."

Given his deep familiarity with these authors, I was interested in how Eric saw his own faith influencing his scientific work. He technically identifies as a biophysicist since his research blends physics with biology and has direct implications for medicine and health.

What drew me [to this topic] is certainly that health aspect. There's a pretty easy connection . . . okay, we're studying biology; that's related to health. So, it's like how do we fight disease and improve the world, bringing God's kingdom into the world through a greater understanding of these pieces to further human welfare and well-being.

His faith also influenced the type of career Eric desired. He told me he had little interest in becoming a physics professor. He had recently interviewed for a job with a private-sector company and was hopeful that he would receive a job offer. In discussing his future career, Eric said, "I want to be able to be equipped to be the best I can be to provide as much support as I can to, say, my church or my community." He explained that part of this equipping is financial in nature, as a job in industry might provide more financial resources that he could use to support his congregation and community. But it is also about the type of life he wants, and "being a supportive person without having a job that works really long hours."

For Eric, religion had provided guidance on crucial questions that face many science grad students, whether or not they are religious: What is the purpose in doing all of this scientific training and education? Is being a scientist "special," or is it just a job like any other? Will my work as a scientist be the central force in my life choices? What does a successful life as a scientist look like? Will my success as a scientist shape how I think about my own worth? If not, how does being a scientist relate to the other parts of my life?

This chapter explores how grad students think about their education and training, how they view their future careers in science, and how they see their scientific endeavors as relating to their sense of self, as well as how some students' religion might influence answers to these questions.

More Than Science

It would be difficult to accuse someone like Eric of lacking a passion for science. Yet, at least in part due to his religious faith, he is making an intentional decision not to take the path toward a research-intensive academic career that many of his faculty and peers see as the most prestigious and ideal career outcome. Several of the religious students I interviewed seemed to be making similar calculations based on their faith. A chemistry student explained that he did not see himself pursuing an academic research career:

> There's plenty of professors for whom work is one of the most important things in their lives, so they're going to always go to the best institute they can, the highest positions they can get to, which is fine. But I'm realizing that's not me . . . it's not something I feel like is kind of the point to life, and what it is that we're here for, and what it is that our spirituality really leads us toward.[2]

To be clear, this student did not dislike research or academia. If anything, his interest in that career path had grown in grad school. He explained:

> I thought I'd always be just a teacher and not do any research, and to me grad school is like so you've got to do research because you have to get the

PhD, but then you can always go after that to some other job where you don't have to ever do research again. But, as I got into grad school and started doing it, I was like, this stuff is amazing.

The issue for this student was primarily about the weight that any potential academic research career might have in making life decisions.

A biology student made these connections even more explicit, telling me,

> So, because of my faith and religion, I think being successful in my career is less important to me than it is to some of my peers. Because for me, to feel like I'm happy and fulfilled in my life, I don't feel like I need to reach the highest levels of science. I don't feel like I need to be a professor at a top university and be publishing in all of the top journals all of the time.[3]

Implied in these students' statements is the idea that being a scientist might not be these students' central identity or the main way they think of themselves and assess their life. A couple of religious students made it explicit that their faith shaped their hierarchy of identities. A Christian sociology student told me, "My role is first and foremost a daughter, a sister, someone in a family, someone's friend. And then it's a graduate student."[4] Similarly, a Christian psychology student stated directly that her religious identity is her "main identity . . . it's what I use to guide myself." She felt that this distinguished her from many of her peers, who viewed grad school and their future scientific careers as the main driver of their identity and actions. When I asked this student about her future career plans, she told me that the church she attends "does church planting" and she would like to seek a job that is near one of those churches.[5]

My survey data also provide some indication that the most religious students, at least, do not put as much weight on their scientific pursuits when assessing their goals and self-image. For instance, as Table 5.1 shows, I asked students their level of agreement with the statement,

TABLE 5.1 Importance of Being a Scientist to a Student's Self-Worth, by Religiosity

Percent Agreeing	Independently of whether you attend religious services or not, would you say you are . . .				
	Very religious	Moderately religious	Slightly religious	Not a religious person	Overall
Being in this program is important to my sense of what kind of person I am.[a]	52%	62%	68%	68%	66%
Overall, being a scientist has a lot to do with how I feel about myself.[b]	46%	56%	61%	65%	62%

a. Pearson's correlation = -0.09, $p < .01$ (note: utilizing all five responses for agreement variable)
b. Pearson's correlation = -0.10, $p < .01$ (note: utilizing all five responses for agreement variable)

"Being in this program is important to my sense of what kind of person I am." Sixty-eight percent of nonreligious and slightly religious students agreed with this statement. This drops to 62 percent among moderately religious students and 52 percent among very religious students. I also asked the students' level of agreement with the statement, "Overall, being a scientist has a lot to do with how I feel about myself." Sixty-five percent of nonreligious students agreed with this statement. This drops to 61 percent among slightly religious students, 56 percent among moderately religious students, and 46 percent among very religious students.

Whether it is a bad thing that religious students place less weight on their scientific endeavors when assessing their self-worth and life goals is a matter of perspective. Undoubtedly, some graduate program directors and faculty advisors want students who are putting all of their personal and professional chips into becoming world-renowned university scientists. At the same time, there are perpetual calls within the scientific and larger academic communities to achieve greater work–life balance and for scientists to see value in activities beyond their research, including teaching, outreach, and service.[6] These students' religious lives appear to be providing a counterbalance that many academic scientists are seeking.

A Focus on People

In their study of natural and social science faculty at top research universities, the sociologists Elaine Howard Ecklund and Elizabeth Long found a group of scientists who connected their faith to an emphasis on "other-directed" activities. Some of these "spiritually engaged" scientists saw themselves as putting more effort toward service-related activities like teaching or scientifically based community outreach than their research-focused peers. Others saw their scientific research as more directly grounded in a desire to help others.[7] This theme came up with several of the religious students I spoke with, as they described how they saw their faith as motivating them to put an emphasis on serving people both in their personal lives and in their careers.

In some cases, this focus on serving people influenced students' thinking about their role as science teachers. I asked a sociology student, for example, how she saw her faith influencing her scientific pursuits:

I think were it not for my religion and spiritual identity, I would not be doing what I am. I see [sociology and Christianity] as having the similar goal of trying to understand people and help them. And help the world, right? My purpose is to make the lives of those around me better.

This student had just started teaching a class focused on sociological research about key social problems, like poverty. She saw potential for this shared mission to be embodied in the classroom.

I just started actually teaching a class yesterday and the students are like, "We like it when professors are encouraging and relate the information to things that we know and understand." And I'm like, 'Geez guys, that's a big ask for me to make social problems encouraging.' But as I thought about it, the examples that I use and the way that I model how to think about things . . . I can touch those students' lives in ways that other people couldn't.[8]

For some religious students, the lives they want to influence were outside of college classrooms. A physics student told me,

> I think of myself as a professional and also as a practicing Catholic. I don't think they're mutually exclusive. The things that I find valuable about my religious and spiritual life are actually largely based on the [attempt] to build a coherent case for understanding life. What does it mean to be human and what does it mean to be a part of a society?[9]

In part due to his faith-infused interest in questions of humanity and society, this student saw himself as aiming to work in science communication and policy where he thought those interests would be better put into action:

> I entered graduate school knowing I didn't want to do research for the rest of my life. And I'll leave graduate school knowing I don't want to do research for the rest of my life. I am much more interested in working on something like either science communication or teaching, or more recently I've actually been considering a lot more trying to move maybe into scientific policy.

Like Eric at the beginning of this chapter, several religious students connected their faith to their research, which they saw as being motivated by a desire to help people, although this took different forms, depending on the discipline. For Eric and other natural science students, this often meant connecting their faith to their interest in research with potential medical or health implications. For social science students, this often meant conducting research that might help particular disadvantaged populations in one way or another. A Christian psychology student, whose research focuses on coping and resiliency among disadvantaged youth, explained to me early on in our conversation that she viewed herself not just as a researcher but also as an applied scholar [and] somebody who's very social justice oriented. . . . There's so many different ways I can be doing the work that I want to do. I could've been a filmmaker or social worker, or I could be a teacher to impact kids and to help kids. There's so many different ways, but I feel like there's some sort of divine purpose in why I'm here, that something brought me to this particular space.[10]

Other religious students discussed a sense of responsibility to use their positions as scientists to advocate for policies that would benefit people. A Jewish sociology student explained it this way:

Some people might put this in terms of, religion is a way to understand God, but to me, the concept of God is best understood as this . . . all tendencies in the universe toward goodness, happiness, light. So justice and goodness are at the heart of where I want to go in life, the things that I'm committed to, my political commitment, what I want to use my platform for, what I want to use my teaching for, the things that I'll continue to fight for.[11]

It might be tempting to dismiss all of this as posturing or ex post facto rationalizations. But a sizable scientific literature suggests that religious beliefs are linked to an individual's motivation for and likelihood of helping others.[12] Of course, this does not mean that religion is the only potential motivation for a scientist to focus on helping people or humanity through their teaching, research, or service.[13] Many of the religious students quoted above acknowledged that they did not think they were the only ones who thought about their work or lives in this way, and some nonreligious students undoubtedly hold similar sentiments. Indeed, a sociology student I interviewed who described her religious identity as fluctuating between agnostic and atheist expressed a similar people-focused ethos. She told me,

I find purpose in my work, and the idea that I'm able to impact people and change people's perspectives through teaching. I don't know if that's necessarily my life's purpose. I think we're all just kind of here, try-ing to do something that makes time go by, but I find purpose in my teaching and my research and through impacting others. So, through interactions with others, through relationships, is what I would say I find meaning in.[14]

Even so, the connection religious students make between their faith and their focus on people—whether in their classrooms, labs, or communities—suggests that religion and spirituality may be a particu-larly powerful influence on how students think and approach their sci-entific work.

Ethics and Faith

Several of the religious students I interviewed also made a connection between their faith and how they understand their approach to acting ethically in the course of their research and interactions with others. Catherine, the Catholic psychology student we met at the beginning of the previous chapter, told me the following when I asked whether and how her faith influenced her work as a scientist:

> There are lots of times I think in research where you can get away with being ethically shady. You can maybe not pay people when you say that you're going to, or take credit for something that's really not your idea. There are just lots of ways to be a jerk. And I think having this underly-ing compass, like strong religious compass that is honed and sort of de-rusted every Sunday or as often as I'm able to engage with my religion is extremely helpful in this environment where . . . it's sort of amoral.[15]

In her book, *Why Science and Faith Need Each Other*, Elaine Howard Ecklund points to a concept of "relational humility" that she has often found to be particularly strong among religious scientists whom she has interviewed. As Ecklund observes, these scientists frequently point to their faith to emphasize how it is "important to ensure that those around them are being treated with care and respect. They view their coworkers and students as people who are created in the image of God."[16] Catherine's focus on how she treats others in the course of her work—not being a jerk, as she puts it—also came up in a conversation I had with a Christian chemistry student:

> I guess in my mind how people work on things is strongly dependent upon their worldview, and what's kind of flavoring the way you look at things. For me, as someone who is actually very spiritual, it certainly guides how I interact with people, whether it's working with coworkers, or whether it's being a manager over other people, I think those stem from a lot of my beliefs. Not to say that people who aren't spiritual aren't ethical, but there's definitely a more uniform code, I guess, of ethics.[17]

Like this student, the other religious students I spoke with were often quick to clarify that they did not think that their nonreligious peers or faculty were inherently unethical or that religious scientists were immune from ethical lapses (Ecklund acknowledges this in her book, as well). Yet the faith to which these students adhere provides a ready-made guide for how they want to treat others.

Religion, Ritual, and Effort

Earlier in this chapter, we saw that some religious students place less emphasis on their scientific work and career when assessing their self-worth because of their faith. This may give the impression that religious students are more lackadaisical or less engaged in advancing in their graduate programs, but this is not accurate according to my interviews with these students. Simply having a more balanced perspective towards one's identity and work life does not mean that these students are putting less effort or time towards their graduate programs or careers. In fact, several religious students expressed that they view their faith as amplifying their effort and focus, rather than reducing it. A Christian biology student, for example, told me,

> Without getting into too much detail about Christian theology, part of being a good religious individual in my particular religious tradition is that you work as hard as you can, and you do your best in the position. Being religious is neither an excuse to refuse a superior nor is it an excuse to slack off because there's a promise of an afterlife.[18]

This student is expressing a connection between theology and work ethic that social scientists have long been interested in documenting. The classic argument is that certain theological concepts within strains of Protestantism led to work-related behaviors that gave rise to entrepreneurial endeavors and capitalistic structures.[19] Subsequent research has found that religiosity can often be positively connected to individuals' expression and embodiment of a strong work ethic regardless of their particular religious tradition.[20] Indeed, a Hindu physics student expressed a similar, theologically derived emphasis on hard work, even to the point of enduring discomfort:

> I think that if there is an objective and I'm working day and night for it and I'm enduring a little bit of suffering in the pursuit of the objective, I see that as a good thing. Now, it's come to my attention that some people actually don't really see enduring pain in a possible goal as necessarily a good thing. But, it seems to me, perhaps that is connected to the religious values that I was brought up with.[21]

Many graduate students struggle with a lack of structure in their programs. While students may have scheduled classes for their first year or two, much of a graduate student's time is unrestricted. Of course, they have research to conduct and sometimes classes to teach, but there is often no set work schedule to follow or time clock to punch into. This apparent freedom makes it is easy for students to struggle with sorting out their "free time" from their "work time."[22] A physics student described his blunt and brief introduction to his program: "I came here and they're like, 'All right, here's your office. You should probably set some appointments up with some people. See you around.' What the hell? There was a tremendous amount of freedom."[23] A biology student likewise described his program as offering a "terrifying degree of freedom" around what students are doing at any particular time.[24]

For some students, this freedom means that they do not spend enough time on their studies and work. A few religious students I spoke with, though, spoke about how they connected their faith to a structured or even ritualistic approach to their studies and work. A chemistry student, for instance, said,

> In graduate school you don't really have a set schedule, and so you can regiment yourself very strongly or you cannot. To me, my [religious] beliefs really kind of infuse into . . . how do I set goals for myself, how to achieve those goals? Those are all more of my own personal discipline of showing up on time, doing things well, that sort of thing.[25]

For other students, the unstructured nature of graduate school means that they do not spend enough time on their personal lives, whether that is family, recreation, or general well-being.[26] Here again, a few religious students mentioned how their faith helps to structure their lives outside of work. A Jewish sociology student, for instance, described how he has benefitted from observing a day of rest:

> I feel like, especially when you're done with classes, you can always justify doing work, right? You always feel like you're not doing enough. But starting Friday sundown to Saturday sundown is Shabbat, and I observe it. I think that was, not only was it a good cultural decision, but it was a very good professional decision that I made, in just forcing myself to not work and then not feel guilty. It's the day of rest, and you've got to really just enjoy living, enjoy your relationships, as the Torah commanded.[27]

For some students, religious rituals help them cope with the challenges presented by their graduate programs and by their lives in general. One biology student, for instance, shared with me how he struggled early in his program with alcohol abuse, a struggle that he overcame in part due to religious rituals:

> Religion was definitely important for me quitting . . . because I was able to build daily rituals around not drinking and the ones where I had rituals for drinking before. So, for example, there is an altar at my house where I light a tea candle every day just as a devotional practice. Here's another one . . . I bake bread every day as a kind of [connection] between the microbial ecology of yeast and the kind of practice of hearth and home and divinity of domestic life. Those kinds of dedicated practices have been very important for me.[28]

As this chapter has shown, science graduate students' questions of purpose and meaning can be found not only in their overarching understanding of their careers and identity, but also in the daily rituals in which they engage. While religion is by no means the only framework that can be used to build these understandings and rituals, it is a particularly powerful one. One area of purpose and meaning that many students grapple with—religious or not—is how or whether to pursue family lives in the context of their scientific careers. The next chapter explores this issue in depth.

6

Family and Career

Sarah

Sarah, who was in her second year of a sociology PhD program, considered herself different from most of the other students, for a number of reasons. One of these is that she identified as a Christian and attended a Christian school for much of her childhood and teenage years. "I was raised in a Baptist church. We were in church all the time, like Wednesdays, Thursdays, Saturdays, Sundays. So very important, we were very involved," she told me. While working on her PhD, Sarah found it difficult to find the time to be as active in a religious community as she would have liked, but she hoped that would change. Like many religious students I talked to, Sarah felt that religion, particularly Christianity, was viewed negatively within her department. "It just seems like in academia you have to be in the closet as a Christian. People don't think of you as intellectually rigorous when those are your beliefs. It's quite a thing in class when people talk about religion, and they talk about it in a really derogatory way."[1]

In addition to her religious beliefs, Sarah also felt distinct from her peers because she was older and had more work experience outside of academia. Before entering the graduate program, she had worked for nearly a decade at various government agencies focused on domestic and international development work. She told me that she might incorporate this topic into her dissertation in some way, but she warned that "the proposal hasn't even been written."

Sarah was also married and had a young child. She described her overwhelmingly younger, single, childless peers as "nice," but ultimately their situations were different from hers. "We have lunch, but when they go hang out at night, I have no idea." Sarah was actually pregnant when she applied to graduate school, and her family shaped both her motivation to go back to school and the schools she could apply to. She told me that her previous job led her to travel frequently, which motivated her to pursue a PhD program once she found out she was pregnant. "I used to be gone almost every other month. Sometimes for a week, sometimes for three weeks . . . you just never know. I knew I wouldn't be able to travel like that anymore." Sarah saw obtaining a PhD as a way to eventually work for similar types of development agencies, but in a position requiring less travel.

As might be expected, her husband and child were significant influences on Sarah's decision-making about where to go to graduate school. "My family and I were living in [this state] before I applied, and so I wanted to go to this school because I didn't want to travel too far away from them." Moreover, she specifically chose the sociology PhD program over a couple of other PhD programs at the same university because she viewed the program as more flexible and family friendly than the others.

Overall, her initial impression of the department's positive culture around family life proved accurate. This does not mean there were no issues or awkward interactions, which she attributed to her family life:

> I had to bring my daughter in once on the weekend to print something and I ran into two faculty members, and they just were really uncomfortable being around a kid. So things like that were like not everybody's cool with it and there are people who I would have wanted to work with because their work aligns well with mine, but they just really are not family friendly.

Tensions surrounding family life and work life are a well-recognized problem in the sciences.[2] Research and interventions focused on such work–family conflict tend to be focused on the role of gender, as women scientists tend to suffer disproportionately from such conflicts.[3] Given many scientific disciplines' desire to increase the number of women in their ranks, addressing and alleviating such work–family conflicts is a major concern.

Compared to gender, though, almost no attention has been paid to the role that religion might have for scientists in work–family tensions and decision-making. On the one hand, this omission is odd, given that a great number of studies have examined the role of religion in shaping individuals' attitudes and behaviors as they relate to family life. On the other hand, it is perfectly in line with the prevailing silence surrounding the role of religion in the lives of scientists. In fact, acknowledging the role of religious beliefs in scientists' family lives might be seen by many as a double penalty. It is bad enough if a scientist loses focus from their research to have a child or get married. That professional sin is made worse if the decision was influenced by something as unscientific as religion.

This chapter considers how religion factors into emerging scientists' family life during graduate school and how religion influences their future decision-making around family and career.

Grad School, Science, and Family Formation

An individual working toward establishing a career as a scientist, particularly as an academic scientist at a prominent research university, faces a number of practical and cultural obstacles to forming a family. On the cultural side, there is a persistent romanticized image of a scientist who maintains an almost monastic life in pursuit of discovery.[4] Getting married and having kids can be seen as a betrayal of what a scientist's true love should be. Consider that, as Albert Einstein gained recognition in the scientific world, he largely abandoned his first wife and his children and made sure his second wife largely accepted that she was secondary to his career. His treatment of his family is often presented with a simultaneous mix of condemnation for his behavior and admiration for his dedication to science. A biographer once wrote, "One of [Einstein's] strengths as a thinker, if not as a parent, was that he had the ability, and the inclination, to tune out all distractions, a category that to him sometimes included his children and family."[5]

On the practical side, the path to becoming a scientist is long and demanding. Let us assume that an individual begins a PhD program immediately after completing their bachelor's degree. That means that they would likely start their program around twenty-two years of age. Although it is possible to complete a PhD in five years, data show that the median time to completion is actually closer to seven or eight years depending on the specific discipline.[6] So, a student is likely to obtain their PhD around twenty-eight or twenty-nine years of age. Given that the median age of first marriage and first birth is around twenty-seven years of age, this does not put these newly minted science PhDs too far behind if they felt that they were in a place to immediately form a family as they leave their graduate programs. Unfortunately, this is often not the case, especially for scientists who want to enter academia. This is because they often have at least one and often multiple postdoctoral positions facing them before they obtain a tenure-track position.[7]

Even if a student is fortunate enough to immediately obtain a tenure-track position, they are looking at about six or more years of being on the "tenure clock" where they are expected to churn out grant proposals and publications, teach their own classes (sometimes for the first time), and be active members in their departments, universities, and disciplinary communities. Indeed, their future employment and career explicitly depends on how successful they are at these activities during this time period.

A physics student neatly summarized this timeline in my conversation with him:

I think I could be a good research professor. I will apply for post docs, for sure. I'm not going to count my chickens before they hatch, right? If I get one job offer I'll be taking that job offer. I think a postdoctoral position would be fun. But I don't think it's conducive to settling down and having a family. I spend two to three years doing one post doc, two or three years doing another post doc elsewhere. Just moving around. So six years, maybe I'll find a position that might allow me to settle down in one spot, and I'm still working like crazy to get tenure. By that point I'm forty, forty-one. And I'm like, eh, next.[8]

As this student noted at the end of this quotation, many scientists are in their late thirties or early forties before they become tenured professors and may feel ready to devote time to their family lives (setting aside any desire for additional promotions and career advancement). This puts particular time pressure on having children, and research finds that scientists tend to ultimately have fewer children than they desire.[9]

The question of when to have children was raised by many of the students I spoke with, especially by women. For instance, a psychology student described her struggle around when to have children and the seemingly "no good time" to do so:

When to have kids is a huge question. My advisor waited to have kids until the last two years, actually. So, right before she got tenure. I actually did two different bachelor's, back to back. So I ended up doing eight years of undergraduate and now I'm doing seven years of grad school and then three years [of a post-doc] . . .

It's a lot, it's a lot. I don't think I'm going to be able to wait as long as her. So it's just figuring out then what will be the best. Probably when I'm a post-doc will be the best . . . this is terrible, but people are like, "There's really no good time to have kids in academia."[10]

Other students mentioned receiving explicit advice to avoid having children. A different psychology student told me,

I definitely want to have children. I've always wanted to have children. There are obviously a lot of female academics with children, but it looks really hard. It looks really hard. And the two professors on our floor who have children, they're like, "Don't do it." And I'm like, well, yeah, everybody says that.[11]

A chemistry student received similar blunt feedback about the challenges of work–life balance as a research-focused academic scientist:

I've talked to women professors specifically that have a family and have kids, and their outlook is not the most positive, which makes it even harder. I was speaking to [a female professor] and I was like, "how do you do it?" Because she has a little kid, and I was like, "How do you balance it?" She was like, "I don't. I feel like I fail every day at everything that I do, and I miss moments at home, and I miss moments at work, and I just feel like I'm not succeeding because this is a field that does not reward average. You either are stellar or you're a failure."

In terms of what she felt, I was like, "thank you for your honesty." But you know, it's kind of like, what do you do with that?[12]

Sometimes this advice is more indirect. A male sociology student recounted to me, "I've heard comments from graduate students and professors who are against students with children, and talking about parents and their children as being inconvenient or a problem or shouldn't be around the department."

Of course, individuals *can* get married or have children during their graduate programs, or during a postdoc, or while an untenured faculty member. Doing so, though, adds another layer of stress and complexity to an already high-stress period. Family-friendly policies and resources tend to be more prevalent for faculty than graduate students, but some universities have taken steps to become more accommodating to graduate students with families.[13]

Even with such resources, though, it can be difficult to balance the demands of a nascent scientific career and the demands of being a parent. Even a generous paid parental-leave policy will typically only help for a few months, and then it is back to the grindstone—now with a young child in tow. A colleague with young children once told me that he does his best research from two to four in the morning because that is when his house is quiet. This might explain why a study found that scientists frequently access online research databases at odd hours at night, on holidays, and on weekends.[14]

It is perhaps not surprising, then, that research shows becoming a parent is strongly associated with scientists leaving their careers in science, especially for women.[15] These concerns were particularly acute for a sociology student who was pregnant when I spoke with her:

> That is something that I've been thinking about a lot. Actually getting toward the end and trying to think about what I actually want to do. And also I should say I'm pregnant. Trying to think about now having a family and trying to be like, "Well, how do I balance academia and family?"
>
> I don't know. I'm really struggling because I'd like to stay in academia. I think it would be really wonderful. I'd enjoy researching and really enjoy teaching. But I also don't know if that's going to be something that's sustainable, if it's going to work. So, I've been starting to think more about what options do I have to go into if I wanted to like . . . if I leave academia. I think it's kind of my priorities are starting to shift a little bit. Yeah. I think it's kind of I'm unsure where I'm going to go.[16]

As if all of this is not enough, the situation becomes even more complex if a student is in a relationship with another scientist, especially another scientist who also wants to become a professor. In this situation, the couple must also worry about how they will both find the jobs they want in the same location, which is extremely difficult given the nature of the academic job market.[17] One student I spoke with shared with me her thoughts and struggles with her pending "dual-career" or "two-body" problem:

> So I mean, the biggest problem is that I'm married [to another science graduate student], and we have to find jobs where we can both be fulfilled

and live in the same place. We spent four years living across country from one another. That was fine. That was worth it, but I'm not doing that anymore. We also plan on having children. And it's unclear to me how any woman with a job is supposed to do this task, so I worry about that.[18]

Whether related to dual-career issues or the timing of having children, science graduate students who place importance on their current or future family life face a daunting path. This is true whether a student is religious or not. But, as we will see, religious students are more likely to find themselves on this path and at an earlier time in their scientific education because their religious values influence the importance they place on their family lives.

Science, Religion, and Family Formation

Although likely not the first thing that comes to mind when thinking of the connections between religion and science, it should not be particularly surprising that science students' religiosity would influence their family-related attitudes and behaviors. A vast amount of research has documented that religiosity is associated with the importance individuals place on getting married and having children. This is not simply an attitudinal correlation either: religious individuals tend to actually get married and have children at a younger age.[19]

My survey of graduate students also shows strong connections between students' religiosity and their current family status. Table 6.1 shows students' responses to a question about their current relationship and parental status. In terms of being in committed relationships, the survey does not find substantial differences across the religiosity groups. Thirty-six percent of nonreligious students say they are not in any type of committed relationship, as compared to 40 percent of very religious students. When looking at the percentage of students who are married, though, we see much larger differences. Forty-three percent of students who identify as very religious are currently married, while 40 percent of

TABLE 6.1 Current Marital and Parental Status, by Religiosity

Are you married or in a committed relationship?	Student Religiosity				
	Very religious	Moderately religious	Slightly religious	Not a religious person	Overall
Yes, I am married	43%	40%	18%	20%	24%
Yes, I am in a committed relationship	17%	27%	46%	44%	40%
No, I do not have a spouse or partner	40%	33%	36%	36%	36%
Total	100%	100%	100%	100%	100%
How many children have you had?	Very religious	Moderately religious	Slightly religious	Not a religious person	Overall
None	77%	88%	93%	94%	92%
1 or more	23%	12%	7%	6%	7%
Total	100%	100%	100%	100%	100%

Note: Marital status and number of children both statistically significant differences at $p<.05$ (Pearson design-based F-test).

moderately religious students are currently married, as compared to less than 20 percent of slightly religious and nonreligious students.

We see a similar pattern when looking at parental status, as shown at the bottom of Table 6.1. Almost 25 percent of very religious students and 12 percent of moderately religious students have at least one child, as compared to 6 percent of the nonreligious students.[20] In short, religious graduate students are at least twice as likely to be married and have a child. Interestingly, the average age of students does not significantly differ across religiosity. The mean age of a very religious student is 28.4 years, as compared to 28.5 for nonreligious students. This suggests that religious students are simply forming families earlier than their graduate school peers rather than coming back to graduate school as older students.

Religious students' intentions concerning having children in the future are also greater than their nonreligious peers' intentions, as can be seen in Table 6.2. We see, for instance, that 22 percent of the nonreligious students said that they intend to have no additional children. If we combine this with the pattern seen in Table 6.1, this means that a sizable proportion of the nonreligious students did not have children at the time of the survey and did not plan to have children in the future. We see, however, that students' intended fertility increases with their religiosity. Sixty-nine percent of very religious students and 62 percent of moderately religious students said they want to have at least two children in the future.

Family Goals versus Career Goals

Religious graduate students in science are more likely to contend with work–family tensions because they are more likely to be married, have children, or want those things in the future. This is directly connected to the importance that religious students place on family. My survey asked students to rate how important "having children" and "having a satisfying marriage or partnership" is to them. As seen in Table 6.3, religiosity is strongly associated with students saying these family goals are very important to them.

Seventy-five percent of very religious students said that having children is very important to them, as compared to only 29 percent of

TABLE 6.2 Additional Children Desired, by Religiosity

Student Religiosity	Very religious	Moderately religious	Slightly religious	Not a religious person	Overall
	[Not including children already had] How many additional children would you like to have in the future?				
None	6%	4%	14%	22%	17%
1	8%	10%	7%	11%	10%
2	36%	42%	37%	32%	34%
3	22%	16%	12%	6%	9%
4 or more	11%	4%	1%	2%	3%
Don't know	17%	24%	28%	28%	27%
Total	100%	100%	100%	100%	100%

Note: Statistically significant differences at $p<.05$ (Pearson design-based F-test).

TABLE 6.3 Importance of Family and Career Goals, by Religiosity

Percent Saying "Very Important"[a]

How important is . . .	Student Religiosity				
	Very religious	Moderately religious	Slightly religious	Not a religious person	Overall
. . . having children to you?[b]	75%	53%	35%	29%	36%
. . . having a satisfying marriage or partnership to you?[b]	91%	85%	74%	67%	72%
. . . having a high status career to you?	11%	25%	18%	23%	22%
. . . having a prestigious job to you?	11%	25%	17%	21%	20%

a. Responses of not important, a little important, and somewhat important not shown.
b. Differences statistically significant at $p<.05$ (Pearson design-based F-test)

nonreligious students saying that having children is very important to them. We might expect, of course, that students who have children would say that having children is very important to them, and we have already seen that very religious students are more likely to have had at least one child. But this does not explain the difference seen in Table 6.3. Even if we limit responses to those students who have not had children, very religious students are over two and a half times more likely to say that having children is very important to them than nonreligious students are.[21]

Does placing importance on family goals mean that religious students put less importance on their nascent scientific careers? The evidence for this is weak. My survey asked students to rate how important "having a high-status career" and "having a prestigious job" is to them. The percentage of students rating these career-goals as very important is also shown in Table 6.3. Simply glancing at the percentages, we see that very religious students appear less likely to say that these career goals are very important. Eleven percent of very religious students say that having a high prestige or status job is very important to them, which is about half of the percentage seen among students overall. However, analyses show that the difference between these percentages is not statistically significant, meaning that the difference is not large enough for us to be entirely confident that it exists across the entire student population.[22] Even if we were confident that very religious students place less importance on these career goals, this does not seem to apply to moderately religious or slightly religious students. These two groups appear to put largely the same amount of importance on having a high status or prestige career as nonreligious students.

In sum, while religious graduate students in the sciences do not necessarily place less importance on career-related goals, they do clearly place more importance on family related goals. The latter fact has implications for the types of careers that religious students intend to pursue.

Career Paths

As many advice books and blogs point out, graduate students in the sciences have a variety of career options, especially those who approach their job searches with a bit of creativity and flexibility.[23] Yet becoming an academic scientist—that is, a professor—is often presented as the ideal or optimal outcome for a newly minted science PhD.[24] Some criticize this tendency, given the scarcity of such positions and the difficulty of obtaining one.[25] Despite such criticism, though, there is still a strong tendency to view science jobs that lack the title of "professor" as a consolation prize.

In fact, the assumed ideal goal is actually narrower than simply becoming a professor, as being a professor at a major research university that produces PhDs is seen as more prestigious than being a professor at, say, a teaching-focused college or university that only grants bachelor's or master's degrees. Remember that graduate students acquire their PhDs at major research universities and are mentored by faculty with those positions, so the implicit or explicit message is that such an environment is the pinnacle of the scientific workforce.

The costs of reaching that pinnacle, however, are the demands and pressures that come with acquiring and keeping such a position.

Professors at major research universities are expected to publish at a high rate, acquire external funding (i.e., grants) to financially support their research and their graduate students, and also teach their classes and mentor their graduate students. And the expectations for these outputs have only increased over time.[26] Some of the students I spoke with reflected on seeing the pressures facing their mentors and how it shaped their own thinking about their future careers. A psychology student recounted the anxiety of watching her pre-tenure advisor attempting to acquire research funding.

> Watching my advisor be really stressed about trying to get grants and funding, and then me being stressed and like, "What is that?" All of that was definitely, was a big struggle for me and actually scary. It made me anxious about like, "If I'm a professor one day and I'm going through this grant process." I guess it made me feel more realistic about what to expect.[27]

Another student pursuing a chemistry PhD described frustration with how his advisor's complete dedication to his research and lack of a "personal life" influenced his own experience in graduate school and plans for the future:

> My advisor does not understand personal life whatsoever because he doesn't have a personal life, which is fine. But for someone who had a personal life, it's a bit of a stress where I go home but then I'm called to come back in. For me, I burned myself out within the first two years.[28]

For this student, his experiences watching and interacting with his advisor meant that he did "not want to be in academia" after he graduated. Indeed, studies have found that many graduate students start out with the goal of becoming a professor at a research-intensive university, only to turn away from it specifically because they come to perceive it as meaning that they will need to sacrifice their personal life, especially their family life.[29]

This is where the greater importance placed on family goals by religious students begins to have implications for the types of careers they intend to pursue.[30] If a tenure-track position at a research-focused university is seen as ill-suited to having children or having a satisfying marriage or partnership, students who place importance on those goals may be expected to avoid these positions. This is supported by my survey data. As Table 6.4 shows, if a student says that both having children and a satisfying marriage or partnership are very important to them, they have a 39 percent chance of saying they plan to seek a research-focused tenure-track position. This probability increases as students place less importance on these family goals. If a student says that neither having children nor having a marriage or partnership is important to them, they have a 51 percent chance of saying they plan to pursue the idealized research-focused professorship. This pattern reverses, however, when considering teaching-focused professor positions. Students who place greater importance on family goals are more likely to say they plan to pursue a teaching-focused academic position, which are often perceived to be less demanding, less pressure-driven, and more family friendly.[31]

TABLE 6.4 Career Intentions, by Importance of Family Goals

	How Important are Family Goals?[b]			
Percentage saying "strongly agree" or "agree":[a]	Very Important	Somewhat Important	A little Important	Not Important
I plan to seek a tenure-track academic job at a research university.[c]	39%	43%	47%	51%
I plan to seek a tenure-track academic job at a college that emphasizes teaching more than research.[c]	32%	27%	23%	19%

a. Predicted probabilities estimated from a multinominal logistic regression model predicting intent to pursue different careers as a function of the importance placed on family goals, importance placed on career goals, academic discipline, gender, race, current marital and parental status, number of publications, years in graduate program, and religiosity.
b. Importance of family goals is a scale constructed from responses to importance of having children and having a satisfying marriage or partnership. Importance of career goals is a scale constructed from responses to importance of having a high status career and a prestigious job.
c. Statistically significant differences at $p<.05$

Since we have already seen that religious students are much more likely to say that their family life is important to them, this means that they will be disproportionately affected by this dynamic—not because their religious lives somehow come into theological conflict with being a research-focused scientist—but because the working conditions of that type of career conflict with the type of personal life religious students are aiming to achieve. In my conversation with him, a chemistry student explicitly made connections between his religiosity, ideal personal and family life, and his future career:

> I would like to be at a place like this if possible, but in a very specific geographical area. We'd both love to be near our families. Both of us grew up with our siblings, with our grandparents, with our parents, that sort of thing, so we would love to have the same thing for our family and for our kids.
>
> So, it's something where that would mean I would either have to severely limit myself to a geographical area, which then makes the application process even harder, or then start looking at lower-level things, like okay maybe not a research-intensive university, maybe it is a permanently undergraduate place, or maybe it is an only-teaching place. A lot of those discussions are very much built on our [religious] belief.[32]

An individual with a PhD in a science discipline is likely to end up with job that pays well and has a high status relative to the general population regardless of whether they reach the perceived pinnacle of a tenured professorship at a research university. Still, the potential for religious students to be restricted to or filtered to less prestigious and potentially less well-paid positions within the scientific workforce reflects larger processes of stratification within science. Research on such processes has largely focused on how women and racial or ethnic minorities end up in such lower status science positions.[33]

Interestingly, many actors who might be concerned about stratification within science when it comes to gender and race or ethnicity may not see any inherent issue if that stratification is a result of religion.[34] If a group of students wants to place more importance on their family life than their career because of their religious values, the argument might go, then that is fine but not something that should be of concern to graduate programs, universities, or other actors within science. In short, it is a matter of choice, and such students could choose to simply not have children if they were really committed to their careers.

Of course, this would not be an acceptable conclusion when discussing how a desire for parenthood disproportionately harms women scientists.[35] The recognition that parenthood and family concerns lead many women out of science or filters them to the lower rungs of the scientific workforce spurs funding and policy changes.[36] The difference, of course, is that actors within science care about increasing the number of women in science. This is generally not the case when it comes to religion, whether in terms of increasing the representation of religious students or increasing representation of various religious traditions. Even if we set aside the question of whether the scientific community should care about religious diversity *in and of itself*, religious diversity could very well, I will argue in the conclusion, have implications for some of the types of diversity that the scientific community does clearly care about.

Conclusion

Religion and Diversity in Science

There is broad interest in diversifying the scientific community. This effort consists not only of supporting current scientists who contribute to the existing diversity, but also of attracting and encouraging new people to enter science who would make the community even more inclusive.

In part, this interest is motivated by a sense of justice and equity. Individuals belonging to some groups have faced, and in many cases still do face, stereotypes and hostility within science. Increasing the participation and presence of those groups is a way to challenge those stereotypes and encourage future generations of scientists from those groups. Scientific occupations are also often prestigious and lucrative, so increasing the participation of some groups can be seen as addressing larger issues of economic inequality and mobility.[1]

Other potential motivations for expanding the diversity of the scientific community might be seen as pragmatic or utilitarian. As the economy becomes increasingly dependent on having enough workers with scientific training and skills, it does not make sense to leave large swaths of the population underutilized.[2] Others have argued that increasing diversity in science is likely to improve scientific work, by bringing a variety of perspectives to the laboratory:

when trying to solve complex problems (i.e., the sort of thing scientists are paid to do), progress often results from diverse perspectives. That is, the ability to see the problem differently, not simply 'being smart,' often is the key to a breakthrough. As a result, when groups of intelligent

individuals are working to solve hard problems, *the diversity of the problem solvers matters more than their individual ability.* Thus, *diversity is
not distinct from enhancing overall quality—it is integral to achieving it.*[3]

While there seems to be wide support for advancing and increasing
diversity in science, things get a bit more complicated when the conversation turns to what diversity means. What dimensions of diversity are
relevant to this effort?[4] There is a clear focus on maintaining and enlarg-
ing the number of women and racial or ethnic minorities in science,
particularly Blacks and Latino/as.[5] Beyond these two core dimensions,
some attention has also been paid to supporting and increasing the
presence of disabled individuals in science, as well as those identifying
as sexual or gender minorities and those who come from low-income
backgrounds or who are first-generation college students.[6]

All of these categories—women, racial and ethnic minorities, disabled
individuals, and so forth—are typically seen as representing a *diversity
of people.* Some scholars and observers of higher education, in contrast,
have focused on the need for a *diversity of ideas.* This argument is often
invoked in reference to the liberal political leanings of academics, with
political conservatives arguing that colleges and universities need to increase the range of perspectives they include just as much as the variety
of social categories.[7]

This distinction between diversity of people and diversity of ideas
is in many ways a false dichotomy. Individuals from unique socio-
demographic groups often have unique perspectives and ideas precisely
because they are from those groups. It is debatable, for instance, whether
an individual who is not Black can truly appreciate the experience of
being Black in science or in the United States in general. Generating
a diversity of ideas, then, often demands a diversity of people. Yet it
would also seem to be the case that, if having a diversity of people is
good because it brings heterogeneous perspectives to science, then there
may be diverse perspectives that do not map neatly onto some socio-
demographic group.

Religion strikes at some of the awkwardness and uncertainty regarding the meaning of diversity in science and higher education more generally. Some might be tempted to throw it into the same category as political ideology—a chosen belief system that can be dismissed as irrelevant or even antithetical to efforts at diversity in science, especially the diversity of people. It is not that simple, however.

As many historians and social scientists have pointed out, the lines between religion, race, and ethnicity can often be blurry.[8] Jewish, Muslim, and Hindu groups in the United States have often been "racialized" and treated in the same manner as racial groups by society.[9] Moreover, some individuals see what others might perceive as religious practice or identity as more of an ethnic or cultural expression than a theological one. And religious boundaries tend to overlay racial and ethnic boundaries, as certain racial or ethnic groups disproportionately identify with particular religious traditions.

Religion also has implications for gender diversity in science. Although social scientists debate its causes, they generally recognize that women tend to be more religious on average than men.[10] In short, religion's contribution to the diversity of ideas in science is intertwined with its contribution to the diversity of people.

We can see some of this reality in my own survey of graduate students. Table C.1 shows differences in religiosity by gender among the students. Although the differences are not huge, we do see that female students tend to be somewhat more religious than their male peers. Larger differences are seen across race and ethnicity, though, as shown in Table C.2. Twenty-two percent of Black graduate students in science say they are very religious, while another 22 percent describe themselves as moderately religious. This is two to three times more than the percentages seen among White students. Although the differences are more modest, we also see that Hispanic or Latino students and South Asian students are also somewhat more religious than their White peers.

Diversifying the gender and racial or ethnic composition of the scientific workforce will likely require diversifying the religious composition

TABLE C.1 Science Graduate Student Religiosity, by Gender

. . . would you say you are a very religious person, a moderately religious person, a slightly religious person, or not a religious person?	Student Gender	
	Female	Male
Very religious	7.2%	6.4%
Moderately religious	15.5%	12.0%
Slightly religious	17.2%	11.6%
Not a religious person	60.1%	70.0%
	100%	*100%*

Note: Design-based *F* test statistically significant at $p < .01$; Responses for "another gender" are not shown here.

TABLE C.2 Science Graduate Student Religiosity, by Race or Ethnicity

. . . would you say you are a very religious person, a moderately religious person, a slightly religious person, or not a religious person?	Student Race or Ethnicity					
	White, European, Caucasian	Black, African, Caribbean	Hispanic or Latino	East Asian (e.g., Chinese, Japanese, Korean, Taiwanese)	South Asian (e.g., Indian, Pakistani, Bangladeshi)	Other or Multiple Races
Very religious	7.3%	22.6%	5.0%	2.5%	3.1%	6.5%
Moderately religious	12.3%	22.8%	17.1%	10.3%	33.9%	7.6%
Slightly religious	13.6%	18.6%	22.5%	7.1%	21.1%	18.8%
Not a religious person	66.8%	36.0%	55.4%	80.1%	41.9%	67.1%
	100%	*100%*	*100%*	*100%*	*100%*	*100%*

Note: Design-based *F* test statistically significant at $p < .01$

of that workforce as well. In other words, ignoring or being hostile to the religious diversity of the scientific workforce may harm our ability to achieve diversity along other dimensions.

Raising the topic of religious diversity in science, especially within the context of the diversity of ideas narrative, may raise concerns about the presence of religious claims in the scientific process. Some may ask why we should welcome or accept scientists who promote creationism, attribute divine intervention to their research, or attempt to integrate a theological agenda into their scientific work.

To be honest, I probably would have raised such objections at one point in my life. And my response to this question now is the same as it would have been many years ago: we should not welcome or accept such work or individuals to graduate science programs. This is not about being hostile toward religion, but simply acknowledging that science programs are meant to train students in *science*, not theology. This means that students who apply to such programs need to have basic competency in science and be ready to conduct research within the bounds of science. This is no different from students applying to any other type of program. If a student applied to do advanced study in, say, music, but they made it clear in their application that they do not know anything about music, actually dislike music, or that they are actually looking to train as an engineer, then they would undoubtedly be declined admission for reasons of "fit" as well.

But my research and conversations with students over the years have led me to realize that this type of concern is largely a red herring. I found no evidence that the religious students I surveyed and interviewed are interested in pursuing what might be called "religious science" as it is commonly stereotyped. If they see their faith relating to their science at all, it is more in terms of their own personal sense of meaning and motivation. I saw no evidence that being religious affected how students think about the fundamental logic and methods of science, nor am I convinced in any way that being religious negatively influences a person's ability to contribute to scientific knowledge. In short, we must overcome the idea that having religious diversity in science makes science less scientific.

Religious students may, however, have unique perspectives on the meaning and nature of ethics in science, how science should engage and serve different segments of society, and what it means to have a successful career in science. While these perspectives could sometimes differ from the dominant narratives within science, that is precisely the point of fostering diversity within science—of both people and ideas.

What does it mean to support and foster religious diversity in science? It is actually relatively simple.

#1: Don't Make Assumptions Based on Stereotypes

A faculty member from my graduate program once recounted to me how there had been some skepticism about my application because I was coming from an undergraduate institution whose name—Trinity University—sounded religious. Trinity does in fact have historical roots in the Cumberland Presbyterian Church and does have an on-campus chapel and spiritual life program. But it never felt like a "religious school" when I was a student. There was no required attendance at religious services, no required Bible classes, or any other sense of an overtly religious institution. Indeed, given the fact that I was (and still am) an atheist, such elements would have been a real obstacle to me attending or remaining at such a school.

Nevertheless, the simple fact that this "religious sounding" school was listed on my application led at least part of the admissions committee to hesitate to accept my application out of fear that I might be a devotee of Ken Ham, the well-known Christian fundamentalist founder of Answers in Genesis and the Creationist Museum. (Ironically, it is a common research strategy within sociology to measure discrimination in work and educational settings by using things like school names or extracurricular groups to indicate a person's demographic characteristics on applications and seeing how it affects the response the individual receives.)[11]

The point here is not to persuade anyone that I did not really attend a "religious college" or that I was not personally religious. The point is that graduate admissions committees should be careful not to extend their assumptions about candidates beyond what is presented to them in an application. If my application was otherwise competitive—strong standardized test scores, positive letters of recommendation, a clear personal statement, and so on—then the religious or nonreligious nature of my alma mater, the religious or nonreligious nature of my extracurricular activities, or any other indicator of my religious or nonreligious life should be irrelevant. There should be no divining about a candidate's religious beliefs, especially when that divining is based on fairly overt stereotyping. In the same sense, admissions committees should not attempt to divine the family plans or work commitment of an applicant based on the perceived gender of the applicant.

#2: Don't Ignore Religious Communities When Doing Science Outreach

Many scientists, science educators, and science programs spend significant amounts of their time conducting outreach to the public. This might consist of giving talks to non-scientists or offering science programs for kids. Some of this outreach is meant to educate the public on complex scientific issues, while some is meant to instill scientific curiosity and interest among the next generation of scientists.

Some might be tempted to dismiss religious communities when doing such work. "Why conduct outreach to groups that might be hostile toward or at least skeptical of science or scientists?" they might ask. Let us first acknowledge that such a question paints not only the diversity of religious communities but also the diversity of scientific issues with a very broad brush. But for the sake of argument, let us say that at least some religious groups are more skeptical or hesitant about science in general or about particular scientific issues. Is that not precisely the reason to conduct outreach to those groups? If we found that, say, low-income groups or particular ethnic groups are hesitant or skeptical of science, would that not motivate many scientists and educators to target those groups for outreach?[12]

Even if such outreach to religious communities does not immediately move the needle in terms of attitudes among those communities, it could provide a spark to some of the kids in those communities to pursue their scientific interests and to see themselves as potential scientists. I think back to Emily, the student we met earlier whose interest in biology was sparked by her somewhat random attendance at a science camp. There are undoubtedly more kids in religious congregations whose scientific passions are waiting to be ignited by their inclusion in such efforts. If a scientist is planning such summer camps or afterschool programs, advertising in local places of worship might be a good way to reach out to those communities.

#3: Challenge the Assumption of Antagonistic Atheism

As we saw, many religious students do not enter their graduate programs concerned about how they will be treated because of their faith or how their faith will affect their happiness in their program. However, many of these students do end up encountering a hostile climate. Religious students often feel isolated and alone in their faith. They overhear derogatory comments about their religion specifically or religion in general. Sometimes they are directly attacked because of their religious beliefs or identity. In some cases they feel that their programs do not recognize basic needs or provide accommodations related to their faith.

Most of these issues can be tied to the prevailing assumption that everyone is at least nonreligious if not hostile toward religion. Of course, this assumption is simply false. As we have seen, a sizable minority of science graduate students—about one in five—are quite religious when measured in a variety of ways. Many of the nonreligious students are not overtly hostile toward religion either, and many likely find such hostility to be misguided. Yet, when the only voices speaking out are those expressing hostility toward religion, then this assumption of antagonistic atheism is allowed to prevail.

While this climate may improve if religious students were more vocal and visible, it is not fair to place this burden solely on these students. Instead, graduate programs and faculty should actively challenge language and behaviors that isolate and stigmatize religious students, and actively provide support to such students. For instance, graduate programs could include a list of campus religious student groups and nearby congregations among the resources provided to new students. These small gestures take little effort but subtly signal to religious students that they are recognized and supported.

#4: Recognize Religion Itself as a Beneficial Part of the Diversity of Science

Some may begrudgingly accept the increased representation of religious individuals in science if it means that it increases diversity along other dimensions, such as race and ethnicity. This treats religious diversity as a type of unpalatable trade—eating your broccoli so you can have your ice cream. This approach is problematic on multiple fronts. First, it means that students will likely feel that they are embraced for one part of their identity (e.g., race) while ignored or disdained for others. Rather than treating individuals as whole packages, this approach reduces them to one dimension. This is a recipe for those students to leave science.

This approach also keeps us from seeing religious diversity itself as a valuable contribution to the scientific community. Religious scientists, for instance, represent natural ambassadors to religious communities when conducting scientific outreach. More abstractly, we saw in previous chapters that religious students often have views—on family, career, and what it means to be successful as a scientist and as a human being—than nonreligious students. They tend to place more importance on their family life and goals. Their identities are not as intertwined with their scientific careers. They see helping people—whether students, research subjects, local communities, or society more broadly—as a key motivator for engaging in science. These are values that could be useful to have in departmental meetings and in the laboratory. Indeed, there have been many calls for science to better reflect and integrate these values. And while these views are by no means isolated to religious students, they do seem to exist at a higher rate among religious students because such students draw from their faith when they think about what is important to them.

With this in mind, I end with the words of a psychology student who, after I asked, at the end of our conversation, whether she had anything she would like to share, told me the following:

If we are trying to train the next crop of scientists and further our own science, we can't be scared of religiosity and we can't feel threatened by religious perspectives. I really think that as much as religion has to be able to stand behind what it believes and be able to talk about, or at least accept, science, I think science in the same way has to be willing to accept religion and not just be threatened because there are all these stereotypes about what a religious identity means.

And I would really hope that in the future we grow in making our top tier research institutions more accepting and open and inclusive of people of all sorts of religious identities, because if we are this diverse and inclusive society, and that's what research institutions want to be, we can't be choosy. We can't pick and choose the groups that we want to include.[13]

ACKNOWLEDGMENTS

Any book like this one requires the assistance of many individuals. First, this project was made possible by a grant from the National Science Foundation (Award #1749130). I very much appreciate the support of the National Science Foundation's Sociology Program and its program director at the time of this project, Dr. Joseph Whitmeyer. Similarly, this book would not have been possible without the support of Jennifer Hammer and the NYU Press team.

Ellory Dabbs assisted vitally in collecting both the survey and interview data for this project. Riley Darragh, Sara Guthrie, and Glenn Noble also provided valuable assistance with data collection.

Elaine Howard Ecklund, Kimberly Rios, David Johnson, and Vicki Baker all gave me helpful feedback as I developed the survey instrument and interview guide. They also provided advice throughout the project. More broadly, I want to especially thank Elaine, who has been a valuable colleague and mentor for many years. I hope that this book makes some small contribution to the religion-science research literature she has pioneered.

Katie Corcoran, Brittany Kowalski, and Erin Hudnall collaborated with me on various presentations and papers from this project, which have ultimately helped in developing this book. I always benefit, in particular, from Katie's feedback on my work. Bernie DiGregorio helped read and copyedit early drafts of these chapters.

I also want to thank the formal and informal childcare providers for my daughters, Avery and Sloane, as work such as this would not be possible without their help. This is especially true with the disruptions caused by the COVID-19 pandemic, which intersected the writing of this book.

As always, I could not have accomplished this project without the many forms of support provided by my family, and especially my partner, Lisa Platt.

Finally, I want to thank the graduate students who participated in this study by completing the survey or sitting down for an interview. The opportunity to meet some very interesting and talented members of the next generation of scientists made this project more enjoyable than any other so far in my career.

APPENDIX

Methodology

The survey and interview data presented in this book are the result of research that began in the summer of 2018 and was made possible with a grant from the National Science Foundation (Award # 1749130). Details about this effort are provided in this appendix.

SURVEY

The survey portion of this study began with the development of a survey instrument and the construction of a sample frame. This process took place in the summer and fall of 2018.

Survey Instrument

When possible, the survey instrument mirrored or adapted previously tested questions from existing surveys. Previous surveys led by Elaine Howard Ecklund and her colleagues,[1] as well as surveys led by Martin M. Chemers and his colleagues were particularly useful in the development of my survey.[2] Items related to students' the importance students place on different family and career goals were adapted from work of Barth, Dunlap, and Chappetta (2016) which was itself derived from the Life Goals Scale developed by Roberts and Robins (2000).[3] Items about students' intent to pursue different career tracks were adapted from the American Chemical Society's Graduate Student Survey.[4] Questions about being treated with less respect due to race, religion, or gender were adapted from the Everyday Discrimination Scale.[5] The full survey instrument can be found in a following appendix.

Sample Frame Construction and Sampling

The target population for the survey was biology, physics, chemistry, psychology, and sociology graduate students in departments ranked in the top sixty of their respective disciplines based on *US News and World Report*'s rankings of graduate programs. For each discipline the top sixty departments were stratified into four tiers (i.e., 1–15, 16–30, 31–45, 46–60). Three departments were selected at random from each tier-discipline combination. This resulted in twelve departments being selected per disciplines and sixty departments being selected in total. This is summarized in Table A.1.

After selecting departments, the next stage of the constructed sample focused on building a database of graduate students. Using departments' online directories of people or students, I extracted the names, emails, mailing addresses, phone numbers, and apparent gender (if possible to code) of every graduate student in the department. If a selected department did not list graduate students in a directory then it was replaced at random within the same discipline-tier category. This only occurred in a few cases, however, as most departments list students in a larger directory or had a dedicated listing of graduate students.

TABLE A.1. Selection of Departments from Discipline-Tier Combinations

Program Strata Based on US News Rankings	Number of Physics Departments Selected from Tier	Number of Biology Departments Selected from Tier	Number of Chemistry Departments Selected from Tier	Number of Psychology Departments Selected from Tier	Number of Sociology Departments Selected from Tier	Total From Tier
Tier 1 (Ranks 1–15)	3	3	3	3	3	15
Tier 2 (Ranks 16–30)	3	3	3	3	3	15
Tier 3 (Ranks 31–45)	3	3	3	3	3	15
Tier 4 (Ranks 46–60)	3	3	3	3	3	15
Total From Discipline	12	12	12	12	12	60

In the end, 6,466 students were identified, although some disciplines were larger than others.[6] From the full student sample frame, eight hundred students were selected at random from each discipline for total sample of four thousand students. Note that this represented an oversample of the smaller disciplines.

Survey Administration

Survey fielding began in February of 2019. The survey was administered on the web and all correspondence took place through email. Students first received an advanced email with the following text:

Dear [FIRST NAME],
I am writing to ask for your participation in a confidential web survey designed by myself and researchers at West Virginia University and supported with a grant from the National Science Foundation (Award 1749130). The purpose of this study is to better understand the backgrounds, experiences, and perceptions of graduate students.

Tomorrow we will send you an e-mail which will contain a URL via which you can access the 15-minute web survey. *As a token of our appreciation, you will have the option of receiving a $5 Amazon.com Gift Code after completing the survey.* Please be on the lookout for this email, *including in your spam or junk email folders.*

You are part of an important group of graduate students randomly selected from departments associated with universities in the United States. You were selected for the survey based on a scientific sampling process designed to generalize to the population of graduate students in the country, as well as to subsets of the population, including graduate students of different genders, disciplines, and at different types of institutions. Your participation is thus essential for valid conclusions about the important issues under study.

We emphasize that this is academic research and *all information you provide will be kept strictly confidential* by the project research team

West Virginia University. Your identity will not be disclosed in any findings disseminated from this study.

If you would like to receive the survey at a different email address, please send your preferred email address to gradsurvey@mail.wvu.edu. This study has been reviewed and acknowledged by the Institutional Review Board at West Virginia University (Protocol 1610297576).

Thank you in advance for your participation.

Sincerely,

Christopher P. Scheitle, PI

Assistant Professor of Sociology

West Virginia University

That email was sent out on February 11, 2019. The next day students received a similarly worded email with a link to the survey which was housed on Qualtrics.[7] Two days later, on February 14, a reminder email was sent, and a final reminder was sent a few days after that, on February 19. As noted in the survey correspondence, a $5 gift code to Amazon. com was offered to survey respondents upon completion.

Response Rate, Weighting, and Analysis

In the end, these efforts produced 1,308 complete responses and 83 partial responses, which equates for an overall response rate of 36.1 percent based on the American Association of Public Opinion Research's Definition #4.[8]

Weights were constructed to account for the disproportionate sampling across disciplines and for response patterns across discipline-tier-gender categories. All analyses utilize Stata's *svy* command to note that departments were the primary sampling unit, the stratification of the department tiers, and the use of sampling weights.

Table A.2 shows the proportion of the original invited sample by discipline—precisely 20 percent each—as compared to the percentage of respondents by discipline. Any discipline over 20 percent in the middle column had a better response rate, while those below 20 percent in the middle column had a lower response rate. We see that psychology (24%

TABLE A.2. Proportion of Sample, Unweighted Respondents, and Weighted Respondents by Discipline

Discipline	Sample Frame	Selected Sample Proportion	Unweighted Respondent Proportion	Weighted Respondent Proportion
Biology	21.66%	20%	20.85%	22.16%
Chemistry	28.64%	20%	14.67%	28.07%
Physics	22.25%	20%	17.04%	21.87%
Psychology	14.79%	20%	24.01%	15.10%
Sociology	12.66%	20%	23.44%	12.80%
Total	100%	100%	100%	100%
N	6,466	4,000	1,391	

of respondents) and sociology students (23%) were somewhat more likely to respond to the survey, while chemistry (14.67%) and physics (17%) were somewhat less likely. The third column in this table shows the proportions by discipline once the weighting is taken into account. In other words, this returns the proportions to close to those seen in the sample frame.

INTERVIEWS

A total of sixty-five semi-structured interviews were conducted with select survey respondents. While the interview subjects were selected in an attempt to represent all of the disciplines and a range of religious current and past religious profiles, students who indicated being more religious on the survey were oversampled given the particular focus of this research on these students. Twelve of the interview subjects were in biology, fifteen were in chemistry, thirteen in physics, fifteen in psychology, and eleven in sociology. Students who completed an interview were offered a $20 Amazon.com gift code.

The full interview guide can be found in a following appendix. Interviews were completed both in-person and using video conferencing services (i.e., Skype, Facetime). The in-person interviews were completed at three universities where students across disciplines were represented to minimize travel costs. Interviews were completed by myself or by one of three graduate research assistants. All interviews were recorded and transcribed. These transcriptions were then coded using NVivo software to isolate key themes outlined in the interview guide or additional themes that arose during the interviews.

SURVEY INSTRUMENT

In this survey, we are interested in your experiences and opinions as a graduate student. This is an academic study designed by researchers at West Virginia University and supported by funding from the National Science Foundation (Award 1749130). The survey will cover a variety of topics, reflecting our broad interest in factors shaping individuals' experiences in graduate school.

Your responses will be kept strictly confidential. Your identity will not be disclosed in any findings disseminated from this study nor will your responses be associated with your institution in particular. This study has been acknowledged by the Institutional Review Board at West Virginia University (Protocol 1610297576).

Please click 'Continue' to begin the survey.

First, some general questions about your educational background and current status as a graduate student.

Q1—Which of the following *best* represents the academic discipline of your graduate program?
1. Physics
2. Chemistry
3. Sociology
4. Biology
5. Psychology

6. Other, please specify: _____

7. I am not a graduate student

Q2 [ASK IF Q1 = 7]—Which of the following *best* describes your status?

1. I left graduate school without obtaining a graduate degree.

2. I obtained a master's degree and left graduate school because that was my plan from the beginning.

3. I obtained a master's degree and left graduate school because I decided I no longer wanted to pursue a doctorate.

4. I obtained a doctorate.

5. Other, please specify: _____

Q3—Which of the following *best* describes the graduate program in which you are currently enrolled? Is the program . . .

1. A terminal master's program. That is, the program is designed to end after obtaining a master's degree.

2. A doctoral program. That is, while students might obtain a master's degree as part of the program, it is assumed that students will obtain a doctorate in the same program.

3. Other . . . please specify: _____

Q4—Have you completed a master's degree?

1. No, I do not have a master's degree

2. Yes, I have a master's degree from this same program

3. Yes, I have a master's degree in the same discipline but from a different program from the one I am currently in

4. Yes, I have a master's degree but in a different discipline from my current program

5. Other, please specify: _____

Q5—In total, how many years have you been a graduate student in this program?

1. This is my first year

2. This is my second year

3. This is my third year

4. This is my fourth year

5. This is my fifth year

6. This is my sixth year

7. This is my seventh year

8. This is my eighth or more year

Q6—Which of the following best represents your funding situation *this year*?

1. I do not have funding

2. I have a teaching assistantship, in which I primarily teach or assist faculty with teaching

3. I have a research assistantship, in which I primarily assist with faculty research

4. I have a fellowship that does not require me to teach or assist with faculty research

5. Other, please specify: _____

Q7—Please indicate the number of articles, solo authored or co-authored, that you have published or have had accepted for publication in *refereed journals:*_____

Q8—Were any of the following significant concerns when you were deciding to go to graduate school? *Select all that apply.*

• My parents or family members did not want me to go to graduate school

• I was concerned that I would not get a job after graduate school

• Perception that I would not fit in because of my gender

• Perception that I would not fit in because of my religion

• Perception that I would not fit in because of my race

• I was afraid that I would not be able to have a family

• Other concern, please specify: _____

• None of the above

Q9—Considering *your specific graduate program*, please rate your level of agreement with each statement . . .

• I spend most of my time outside of classes and the office socializing with people from this program.

• I feel like I belong in this program.

- Being in this program is important to my sense of what kind of person I am.
  1. Strongly agree
  2. Agree
  3. Neither agree nor disagree
  4. Disagree
  5. Strongly disagree

Q10—Considering *the academic discipline of your graduate program more broadly*, please rate your level of agreement with each statement . . .
- In general, being in this discipline is an important part of my self-image.
- I have a strong sense of belonging in this discipline's community.
- Being in this discipline is a major factor in my social relationships.
  1. Strongly agree
  2. Agree
  3. Neither agree nor disagree
  4. Disagree
  5. Strongly disagree

Q11—Please rate your level of agreement with each statement . . .
- I have come to think of myself as a scientist.
- Many of my closest friends are scientists.
- Overall, being a scientist has a lot to do with how I feel about myself.
- In a group of scientists, I really feel that I belong
  1. Strongly agree
  2. Agree
  3. Neither agree nor disagree
  4. Disagree
  5. Strongly disagree

Q12—Please indicate the extent to which you are confident you can successfully complete the following tasks:
- Relate results and explanations to the work of others
- Generate a research question to answer

- Publish research in peer-reviewed outlets
  1. Not at all confident
  2. A little confident
  3. Somewhat confident
  4. Very confident

Q13—*Thinking specifically about your experiences as a graduate student*, how often do you feel like you are treated with less respect because of your *gender*?
1. Never
2. Less than once a year
3. A few times a year
4. A few times a month
5. At least once a week
6. Almost every day

Q14—*Thinking specifically about your experiences as a graduate student,* how often do you feel like you are treated with less respect because of your *religion*? If you do not identify with a religion, how often does this happen to you because you *do not identify with a religion*?
1. Never
2. Less than once a year
3. A few times a year
4. A few times a month
5. At least once a week
6. Almost every day

Q15—*Thinking specifically about your experiences as a graduate student*, how often do you feel like you are treated with less respect because of your *race or ethnicity*?
1. Never
2. Less than once a year
3. A few times a year
4. A few times a month
5. At least once a week
6. Almost every day

The following questions concern your personal and professional goals.

Q16—How important is having children to you?
   1. Not important to me
   2. A little important to me
   3. Somewhat important to me
   4. Very important to me

Q17—How important is having a high status career to you?
   1. Not important to me
   2. A little important to me
   3. Somewhat important to me
   4. Very important to me

Q18—How important is having a prestigious job to you?
   1. Not important to me
   2. A little important to me
   3. Somewhat important to me
   4. Very important to me

Q19—How important is having a satisfying marriage or partnership to you?
   1. Not important to me
   2. A little important to me
   3. Somewhat important to me
   4. Very important to me

Please indicate your level of agreement with the following statements:

Q20—I plan to seek a tenure-track academic job at a research university.
   1. Strongly agree
   2. Somewhat agree
   3. Neither agree nor disagree
   4. Somewhat disagree
   5. Strongly disagree

Q21—I plan to seek a tenure-track academic job at a college or university that emphasizes teaching more than research.

1. Strongly agree
2. Somewhat agree
3. Neither agree nor disagree
4. Somewhat disagree
5. Strongly disagree

Q22—I plan to seek a researcher (not professor) job in an academic setting.

1. Strongly agree
2. Somewhat agree
3. Neither agree nor disagree
4. Somewhat disagree
5. Strongly disagree

Q23—I plan to seek a job as a researcher in an industry, government, or nonprofit setting.

1. Strongly agree
2. Somewhat agree
3. Neither agree nor disagree
4. Somewhat disagree
5. Strongly disagree

Q24—I plan to seek a job outside of research.

1. Strongly agree
2. Somewhat agree
3. Neither agree nor disagree
4. Somewhat disagree
5. Strongly disagree

Graduate students often have a primary faculty advisor. This is usually the person who supervises the student's thesis or dissertation.

Q25—How important is it that your primary faculty advisor is of the same race or ethnicity as you?

1. Not important to me
2. A little important to me
3. Somewhat important to me
4. Very important to me

Q26—How important is it that your primary faculty advisor is of the same gender as you?
1. Not important to me
2. A little important to me
3. Somewhat important to me
4. Very important to me

Q27—How important is it that your primary faculty advisor has the same religion as you?
1. Not important to me
2. A little important to me
3. Somewhat important to me
4. Very important to me

Q28—Do you currently have a faculty advisor?
1. Yes
2. No

[ASK IF Q28 = 1] Please indicate your level of agreement with the following statements about your faculty advisor. If you have more than one advisor, think about the one you consider your *primary* advisor.

Q29—"My advisor conveys feelings of respect for me as an individual."
1. Strongly agree
2. Agree
3. Neither agree nor disagree
4. Disagree
5. Strongly disagree

Q30—"My advisor encourages me to prepare for advancement in this program."

    1. Strongly agree

    2. Agree

    3. Neither agree nor disagree

    4. Disagree

    5. Strongly disagree

Q31—"My faculty advisor is available when I need to speak to him or her."

    1. Strongly agree

    2. Agree

    3. Neither agree or disagree

    4. Disagree

    5. Strongly disagree

Q32—To the best of your knowledge, which of the following represents the gender of your primary faculty advisor?

    1. Female

    2. Male

    3. Another gender identity, please specify: _____

Q33—To the best of your knowledge, which of the following represents the race or ethnicity of your primary advisor? Select all that apply.

    1. American Indian or Alaska Native

    2. Black, African, Caribbean

    3. Caucasian, White, European

    4. Central Asian / Arab

    5. East Asian (Chinese, Japanese, Korean, Taiwanese, etc.)

    6. Hispanic or Latino

    7. South Asian (Indian, Pakistani, Bangladeshi, etc.)

    8. Other, please specify: _____

    9. I am not sure

Q34—To the best of your knowledge, what is the professional rank of your primary advisor?

    1. Assistant professor

    2. Associate professor

3. Full professor
4. Distinguished/Endowed/Named professor
5. Other . . . please specify: _____
6. I am not sure

The following questions concern religion and spirituality. **Your responses are important even if you do not consider yourself religious or spiritual.**

Q35—Religiously, do you consider yourself to be Protestant, Catholic, Jewish, Mormon, Muslim, not religious, or something else? If more than one, click the one that **best** describes you:
  1. Protestant
  2. Catholic
  3. Just a Christian
  4. Jewish
  5. Mormon
  6. Muslim
  7. Eastern Orthodox
  8. Buddhist
  9. Hindu
  10. Sikh
  11. Baha'i
  12. Jain
  13. Not religious
  14. Agnostic
  15. Atheist
  16. Something else . . . please specify: _____
Q36 [SKIP IF Q35 = 13, 14, 15]—Do you belong to a particular denomination or tradition within this religion?
  1. No
  2. Yes . . . please specify: _____

Q37—Apart from weddings and funerals, about how often do you attend religious services these days?

1. More than once a week
2. Once a week
3. Once a month
4. Once or twice a year
5. Less than once a year
6. Never

Q38—Independently of whether you attend religious services or not, would you say you are . . .

1. A very religious person
2. A moderately religious person
3. A slightly religious person
4. Not a religious person

Q39—Please indicate which statement below comes closest to expressing what you believe about God. Would you say . . . ?

1. I don't believe in God
2. I don't know whether there is a God and I don't believe there is any way to find out
3. I don't believe in a personal God, but I do believe in a Higher Power of some kind
4. I find myself believing in God some of the time, but not at others
5. While I have doubts, I feel that I do believe in God
6. I know God really exists and I have no doubts about it

Q40—About how often do you spend time praying outside of religious services?

1. Never
2. Less than once a week
3. Once a week
4. Several times a week
5. Once a day
6. Several times a day

Q41—In what religion *were you raised*? Were you raised Protestant, Catholic, Jewish, Mormon, Muslim, not religious, or something else? If more than one, click the one that **best** describes you:
1. Protestant
2. Catholic
3. Just a Christian
4. Jewish
5. Mormon
6. Muslim
7. Eastern Orthodox
8. Buddhist
9. Hindu
10. Sikh
11. Baha'i
12. Jain
13. Not religious
14. Agnostic
15. Atheist
16. Something else . . . please specify: _____

Q42 [SKIP IF Q41 = 13, 14, 15]—*Were you raised* in a particular denomination or tradition within this religion?
1. No
2. Yes . . . please specify: _____

Q43—*At age 16*, independently of whether you attended religious services or not, would you have said you were . . . ?
1. A very religious person
2. A moderately religious person
3. A slightly religious person
4. Not a religious person

Q44—Would you say that your knowledge and training in your discipline has . . . ?
1. Made you become much more religious
2. Made you become slightly more religious

3. Had no effect on how religious you are

4. Made you become slightly less religious

5. Made you become much less religious

Q45—For me personally, my understanding of science and religion can be described as a relationship of . . .

1. Conflict; I consider myself to be on the side of religion.

2. Conflict; I consider myself to be on the side of science.

3. Independence; they refer to different aspects of reality.

4. Collaboration; each can be used to help support the other.

Q46—How much do you agree or disagree with the following statement: "I conceal or camouflage signs of my religious views or identity around people in my graduate program."

1. Strongly agree

2. Agree

3. Neither agree nor disagree

4. Disagree

5. Strongly disagree

Q47—How much do you agree or disagree with the following statement: "In general, I feel that people in my discipline have a negative attitude toward religion."

1. Strongly agree

2. Agree

3. Neither agree nor disagree

4. Disagree

5. Strongly disagree

You are almost done. These last questions are for classification purposes.

Q48—What is the highest educational degree obtained by your mother?

1. Less than high school degree

2. High school degree

3. Associate's degree

4. Bachelor's degree

5. Master's degree

6. PhD

7. Professional degree (e.g., M.D., D.V.M., J.D.)

8. Don't know

9. Does not apply

Q49—What is the highest educational degree obtained by your father?

1. Less than high school degree

2. High school degree

3. Associate's degree

4. Bachelor's degree

5. Master's degree

6. PhD

7. Professional degree (e.g., M.D., D.V.M., J.D.)

8. Don't know

9. Does not apply

Q50—What is the gender that you were assigned at birth?

1. Female

2. Male

3. Other, please specify: _____

Q51—With what gender do you currently identify?

1. Female

2. Male

3. Other, please specify: _____

Q52—What year were you born?

1. [Select from Drop Down Box]

Q53—In what country did you spend the majority of your childhood, that is ages 16 or under?

2. [Select from Drop Down Box]

Q54—Which of the following best describes your US citizenship status?

1. I am a citizen of another country, not the US

2. I was not born in the US, but I am a US citizen

3. I was born in the US, but one of my parents was born in another country

4. I was born in the US, but both of my parents were born in another country

5. I was born in the US and both of my parents were born in the US

Q55—Which of the following best represents your race or ethnicity? Select all that apply.

1. American Indian or Alaska Native

2. Black, African, Caribbean

3. Caucasian, White, European

4. Central Asian / Arab

5. East Asian (Chinese, Japanese, Korean, Taiwanese, etc.)

6. Hispanic or Latino

7. South Asian (Indian, Pakistani, Bangladeshi, etc.)

8. Other, please specify: _____

Q56—Are you married or in a committed relationship?

1. Yes, I am married

2. Yes, I am in a committed relationship

3. No, I do not have a spouse or partner

Q57—How many children have you had?

1. None

2. 1

3. 2

4. 3

5. 4 or more

Q58—How many additional children would you like to have in the future?

1. None

2. 1

3. 2

4. 3

5. 4 or more

6. Don't know

Q59—Would you consider yourself to be . . .

1. Heterosexual
2. Bisexual
3. Gay, lesbian, homosexual
4. Other, please specify: _____

Q60—Where would you place your political views on a seven-point scale, with 1 being "Extremely liberal" and 7 being "Extremely conservative."

1. Very liberal
2. Liberal
3. Slightly liberal
4. Moderate
5. Slightly conservative
6. Conservative
7. Very conservative

Thank you very much for answering all of these questions. We invite a portion of our respondents to take part in a conversation about these topics. Are you willing to be contacted?

1. Yes
2. No

Thank you again for completing this survey. As a token of appreciation, we are happy to send you a $5 Amazon.com Gift Code. To receive this, please provide an email address where you would like us to send the code. You will receive the code in an email from Amazon.com.

Please note that *it may take several days to process and send the code.*

If you do not wish to receive a gift code, then just leave this entry blank.

_____

INTERVIEW GUIDE

Academic and Research Background

To start, could you tell me a little bit about the graduate program you are in and how you came to enter this program?

1. Do you remember when you started thinking about pursuing a graduate degree in this area? Why do you think you picked this discipline rather than some other one? Was there a particularly influential experience or individual?
2. Does anyone in your family have a graduate degree in this or some other area?
3. And in a few sentences, could you describe the general topic or question you are interested in pursuing for your thesis or dissertation research?
4. How did you come to focus in this area?

Professional Identity

One issue we are interested in is how graduate students think of their future professions and themselves.

5. Can you tell me what it means to you to be a [biologist, chemist, etc.]?
6. Do you currently think of yourself as a "biologist" [replace with field], or not? If so, do you remember when you really started to feel like you were a professional in this field? If not, why do you think you don't identify in this way? Is there something or sometime when you think you will?
7. Have there been any particularly influential experiences or individuals that have helped you develop your professional identity?
8. How would you describe your future professional goals?
9. Do you have any concerns that these professional goals might conflict with any personal goals or values you might have? If yes, how so?

10. Your graduate program is in a field that falls under the larger umbrella of science. Do you think of yourself as a scientist? If so, do you remember when you started to feel like or identify as a scientist? If not, why do you think you don't identify in this way? Is there something or sometime when you think you will?

11. What does it mean to you to be a scientist? How do you view the role of science and scientists in society?

Experiences and Discrimination

12. When you were thinking about going to graduate school, did you have any concerns or fears about what you would experience? Can you tell me about those? What made you worried about this?

13. In general, how has your experience been in this program? What has been most challenging, either personally or professionally? Follow-up: Can you describe a recent time when that has been an issue?

14. How would you describe your relationship with the other students in your program? Would you say your cohort/other grad students are your primary friend group?

15. Have you had any negative experiences so far in your graduate program, whether related to those initial fears or entirely different issues? If so, can you tell me about what happened in one of those experiences or give an example?

16. Have you either personally experienced or heard any negative treatment of individuals based on their gender, race or ethnicity, or religion? If so, can you tell me about this?

17. Do you have a primary advisor or mentor in your graduate program? If so, can you tell me a little about your relationship with him/her? How did you come to this relationship? Has it been a positive relationship?

18. Is there a moment where your advisor has been particularly supportive or, maybe, unsupportive? Can you describe what happened?

Views on Connection between Religion, Spirituality and Science
One issue we are specifically interested in what you think about religion [and spirituality] and how they relate to your work, if at all.

19. How do religion and spirituality come up, if at all, in the discourse or broader conversation in your discipline or field?
20. What kinds of informal ways do people in your department talk about religion (during coffee-breaks, at a bar, mealtime conversation)?
21. Can you describe anyone in your field, whether another graduate student or a faculty member, for whom religion and spirituality is very influential? How do you know religion is important to this person? How does it play out in their life?
22. How does religion (or spirituality) influence your professional identity or work as a scientist (or social scientist)?
23. IF RELIGIOUS: Do you feel like your religious identity or beliefs have influenced your scientific interests?
24. IF RELIGIOUS: What about your future personal and professional goals? Do you feel like your religious identity or beliefs shape your goals? If so, how?
25. IF RELIGIOUS: In general, how has your religious identity or beliefs influenced your grad school experience, either positively or negatively?
26. IF RELIGIOUS: How has your religious identity or beliefs influenced your relationships with other students? Do you talk about religion with other students?
27. ASK ALL: Has religion ever come up with your advisor? If yes, how so?
28. IF RELIGIOUS: How has religion shaped your relationship with your advisor?
29. On the other hand, how does being a scientist (social scientist) influence how you think about or view religion?

30. Some say there is a "conflict between science and religion." How would you respond to such a statement? Do you hear people say this? What do you think these people mean?

Personal Religious/Spiritual History and Family Life

Now, I have just a few questions about your own religious history.

31. In what ways was religion a part of your life as a child? How was religion talked about in your family setting?

32. During your school education were there ways you thought about the connection between science and religion?

33. Do you have children? To what extent does religion come up in how you raise them? [Even for those who are not religious] How do you talk with your children about religion?

Current Religious Identity, Beliefs, and Practices

34. How about now for you personally, how would you describe the place of religion or spirituality in your life? [Or: if they have already talked about the place of religion or spirituality in their lives, ask:] Do you have anything more to add about the place of religion or spirituality in your life now?

35. What religious or spiritual beliefs do you hold? How about religious practices? Are there any spiritual or religious practices you engage in?

36. [If religious:] If you have a religious tradition, in what specific way does being part of that religious tradition influence your life now? What kinds of things do you do to practice being part of that religious tradition?

37. [Can skip, if redundant.] Thinking about the arc of your life so far, was there a transition from being religious to not being religious? What were the important influences on this transition? [Alternatively, was there a time when you experienced a dramatic religious shift? What was part of that shift?]

38. How do you answer the big questions of the meaning of life, such as why we are here, what is the meaning of my life? How do you find purpose?

39. Last, did anything I asked [or didn't ask] spark anything else you wanted to mention?

NOTES

INTRODUCTION

1 This and all subsequent quotations attributed to Danielle are from Interview 106 (female; physics, Christian), conducted on March 27, 2019.

2 In recent years, about 1 percent of PhDs in physics were awarded to African Americans, while about 20 percent were awarded to women. Patrick J. Mulvey, Starr Nicholson, and Jack Pold, "Trends in Physics PhDs: Results from the 2019 Survey of Enrollments and Degrees and the Degree Recipient Follow-up Survey for the Classes of 2017 and 2018," *American Institute of Physics* (2021), www.aip.org.

3 Anna Sverdlik, Nathan C. Hall, and Lynn McAlpine, "PhD Imposter Syndrome: Exploring Antecedents, Consequences, and Implications for Doctoral Well-Being." *International Journal of Doctoral Studies* 15 (2020): 737–59; Jerry Coyne, "Yes, There Is a War between Science and Religion," *The Conversation* (December 21, 2018), www.theconversation.com.

4 The sociologists John H. Evans and Michael S. Evans call this the focus on "epistemological conflict" between religion and science. John H. Evans and Michael S. Evans, "Religion and Science: Beyond the Epistemological Conflict Narrative," *Annual Review of Sociology* 34 (2008): 87–105.

5 John H. Evans, "Epistemological and Moral Conflict between Religion and Science," *Journal for the Scientific Study of Religion* 50, no. 4 (2011): 707–27.

6 It is important to also note that sometimes apparent religious sources of rejecting science are actually a product of other factors, such as political conservatism. Research has found that acceptance of climate change is much more driven by an individual's political ideology than their religiosity. See, for instance, Elaine Howard Ecklund, Christopher P. Scheitle, Jared Peifer, and Daniel Bolger, "Examining Links between Religion, Evolution Views, and Climate Change Skepticism," *Environment and Behavior* 49, no. 9 (2017): 985–1006.

7 For instance, see chapter 5 in Elaine Howard Ecklund and Christopher P. Scheitle, *Religion vs. Science: What Religious People Really Think* (New York: Oxford University Press, 2018).

8 This point is made by John Evans in his book *Morals Not Knowledge: Recasting the Contemporary U.S. Conflict between Religion and Science* (Oakland: University of California Press, 2018).

9 For an overview of theory and research on social identity see, for instance: Blake E. Ashforth and Fred Mael, "Social Identity Theory and the Organization,"

Academy of Management Review 14, no. 1 (1989): 20–39; Jan E. Stets and Peter J. Burke, "Identity Theory and Social Identity Theory," *Social Psychology Quarterly* (2000): 224–37; Naomi Ellemers, Russell Spears, and Bertjan Doosje, "Self and Social Identity," *Annual Review of Psychology* 53, no. 1 (2002): 161–86.

10 It is not the case that only occupations requiring advanced education instill strong social identities. For instance, I live in West Virginia where coal mining is connected to a very strong social identity, as seen partially in the many cars and trucks that display stickers stating that the driver is a coal miner or related to a coal miner.

11 The sociologists Timothy L. O'Brien and Shiri Noy have found in their analyses of survey data that individuals' approach to thinking about science and religion tend to cluster with and indicative of a wide-range of other attitudinal and socio-demographic variables. Timothy L. O'Brien and Shiri Noy, "Traditional, Modern, and Post-Secular Perspectives on Science and Religion in the United States," *American Sociological Review* 80, no. 1 (2015): 92–115. See also O'Brien and Noy, "A Nation Divided: Science, Religion, and Public Opinion in the United States," *Socius* 2, no. 1 (2016): 1–15.

12 Gordon Gauchat, "Politicization of Science in the Public Sphere: A Study of Public Trust in the United States, 1974 to 2010," *American Sociological Review* 77, no. 2 (2012): 167–87. Timothy L. O'Brien and Shiri Noy, "Political Identity and Confidence in Science and Religion in the United States," *Sociology of Religion* 81, no. 4 (2020): 439–61.

13 Lauren Griffin, "Why Do Science Issues Seem to Divide Us along Party Lines?" *The Conversation* (October 16, 2016), www.theconversation.com.

14 While it is tempting to see individuals' "conversions" to a new belief system—including a new religion—as the result of some intellectual revelation, sociological research suggests that it is often more the result of changing social ties. That is, individuals become friends with people of a different religion and only later start to identify with that new religion. See, for instance, David A. Snow, Louis A. Zurcher Jr., and Sheldon Ekland-Olson, "Social Networks and Social Movements: A Microstructural Approach to Differential Recruitment," *American Sociological Review* 45, no. 5 (1980): 787–801.

15 See, for instance, Robert S. Broadhead, *The Private Lives and Professional Identity of Medical Students* (New Brunswick, NJ: Transaction Books, 1983); Mitchell J. M. Cohen, Abigail Kay, James M. Youakim, and John M. Balaicuis, "Identity Transformation in Medical Students," *American Journal of Psychoanalysis* 69, no. 1 (2009): 43–52.

16 See Jeff Hardin, Ronald L. Numbers, and Ronald A. Binzley, *The Warfare between Science and Religion: The Idea that Wouldn't Die* (Baltimore, MD: Johns Hopkins University Press, 2018). See also David Baker, "The Great Antagonism That Never Was: Unexpected Affinities between Religion and Science in Post-Secular Society," *Theory and Society* 48 (2019): 39–65.

17   Thomas F. Gieryn, *Cultural Boundaries of Science: Credibility on the Line* (University of Chicago Press, 1999).

18   To be clear, this can and has been a two-way process at times. That is, some religious actors or communities have benefited from doing their own boundary work in relation to science.

19   Robert K. Merton, "A Note on Science and Democracy," *Journal of Legal and Political Sociology* 1 (1942): 115–26.

20   Interview 104 (male, psychology, agnostic), conducted on March 26, 2019.

21   Interview 136 (female, biology, Christian), conducted on May 28, 2019.

22   Interview 151 (male, chemistry, agnostic), conducted on June 13, 2019.

23   Robert K. Merton, "Science and the Social Order," *Philosophy of Science* 5, no. 3 (1938): 321–37.

24   A recent study confirms the perceived counter-stereotypical nature of a religious scientist, especially among atheists. Sharp et al 2021 found in a series of studies that atheists were more likely to see religious scientists as violating the stereotypical nature of a scientist. Given research showing that atheists represent a large proportion of the scientific population, these perceptions are likely quite prominent for religious scientists. See Carissa, A. Sharp, Carola Leicht, Kimberly Rios, Natalia Zarzeczna, and Fern Elsdon-Baker, "Religious Diversity in Science: Stereotypical and Counter-Stereotypical Social Identities," *Group Processes & Intergroup Relations* 25, no. 7 (2021): 1836–60, https://doi.org/10.1177/13684302 20987598.

25   In fact, much of my past work has examined these issues among science faculty. See Elaine Howard Ecklund and Christopher P. Scheitle, "Religion among Academic Scientists: Distinctions, Disciplines, and Demographics," *Social Problems* 54, no. 2 (2007): 289–307; Elaine Howard Ecklund, David R. Johnson, Christopher P. Scheitle, Kirstin R. W. Matthews, and Steven W. Lewis, "Religion among Scientists in International Context: A New Study of Scientists in Eight Regions," *Socius* 2, no. 1 (2016): 1–9; Christopher P. Scheitle and Elaine Howard Ecklund, "Perceptions of Religious Discrimination among US Scientists," *Journal for the Scientific Study of Religion* 57, no. 1 (2018): 139–55.

26   Katherine V. Bruss and Mary Kopala, "Graduate School Training in Psychology: Its Impact upon the Development of Professional Identity," *Psychotherapy: Theory, Research, Practice, Training* 30, no. 4 (1993): 685–91.

27   Volker C. Franke, "Duty, Honor, Country: The Social Identity of West Point Cadets," *Armed Forces & Society* 26, no. 2 (2000): 175–202; Brian Lande, "Breathing Like a Soldier: Culture Incarnate," *Sociological Review* 55, no. s1 (2007): 95–108.

28   Matt Might, "10 Easy Ways to Fail a PhD," blog post, accessed December 30, 2022, matt.might.net; Joan E. Strassmann, "The Monastic Glory of a Seven Year PhD," blog post, November 23, 2014, sociobiology.wordpress.com. When I was accepted to Penn State for my own PhD program, a faculty member there commented that

the university's relatively isolated location in the rural middle part of Pennsylvania gave it a certain "monastic quality," which was attractive when pursuing a PhD.

29 About two percent of the population aged thirty years or older had a doctoral degree in 2020. US Census Bureau, Current Population Survey, 2020 Annual Social and Economic Supplement.

30 Jessica McCrory Calarco, *A Field Guide to Grad School: Uncovering the Hidden Curriculum* (Princeton, NJ: Princeton University Press, 2020).

31 Many PhD programs are designed so that students will obtain a master's degree along the way (often at the end of their second year in the program), while some do not require students to obtain a master's degree at all.

32 For example, see Brigid O'Rourke, "Growing Gap in STEM Supply and Demand," *The Harvard Gazette*, November 18, 2021; Alex West and Peri Becker, "Investing in STEM for Growth in Education and Workforce Development," *Citi Ventures*, October 5, 2021.

33 A couple of the departments selected for the sample appeared to offer terminal master's programs in addition to a PhD program based on their websites, but the overwhelming majority of programs appeared to be PhD-focused. Indeed, on the survey, 98 percent of the students reported that they were in a doctoral program, with the remaining 2 percent of students said they were in a terminal master's program or some other type of program (e.g., dual degree).

34 There is a sizable literature discussing the liminal or in-between state of PhD students. Jeffrey M. Keefer, "Experiencing Doctoral Liminality as a Conceptual Threshold and How Supervisors Can Use It," *Innovations in Education and Teaching International* 52, no. 1 (2015): 17–28; Nicolas Raineri, "Business Doctoral Education as a Liminal Period of Transition: Comparing Theory and Practice," *Critical Perspectives on Accounting* 26, no. 1 (2015): 99–107. Martin Compton and Danielle Tran, "Liminal Space or in Limbo? Post Graduate Researchers and Their Personal Pie Charts of Identity," *Compass: Journal of Learning and Teaching* 10, no. 3 (2017): 1–14.

CHAPTER 1. THE RELIGIOUS LIVES OF SCIENTISTS-IN-TRAINING

1 This and all subsequent quotations attributed to Mark are from Interview 150 (male, chemistry, Christian), conducted on June 13, 2019.

2 This and all subsequent quotations attributed to Adhira are from Interview 168 (female, biology, Hindu), conducted on June 29 2019.

3 See, for example, Joseph O. Baker and Buster G. Smith, "The Nones: Social Characteristics of the Religiously Affiliated," *Social Forces* 87, no. 3 (2009): 1251–63; Laurie Goodstein, "Study Finds One in 6 Follows No Religion," *New York Times*, December 12, 2012; Alan Cooperman and Gregory A. Smith, "The Factors Driving the Growth of Religious 'Nones' in the U.S," *Pew Research Center*, September 14, 2016, www.pewresearch.org.

4 Pew Research Center, "Where Americans Find Meaning in Life," November 20, 2018, www.pewforum.org.

5 Pew Research Center, "The Religious Typology," August 29, 2018, www.pewforum .org.

6 See Bryan Stone, "Religious Faith and Science in *Contact*," *Journal of Religion & Film* 2, no. 2 (1998): 1–10.

7 See Todd V. Lewis and K. Arianna Molloy, "Religious Rhetoric and Satire: Investigating the Comic and Burlesque Frames within *The Big Bang Theory*," *Journal of Media and Religion* 14, no. 2 (2015): 88–101.

8 William H. Swatos Jr. and Kevin J. Christiano, "Secularization Theory: The Course of a Concept," *Sociology of Religion* 60, no. 3 (1999): 209–28; Jeffrey K. Hadden, "Toward Desacralizing Secularization Theory," *Social Forces* 65, no. 3 (1987): 587–611.

9 James H. Leuba, *The Belief in God and Immortality: A Psychological, Anthropological, and Statistical Study* (Boston: Sherman, French & Company, 1916).

10 There were not many national public opinion surveys in the 1910s, and even fewer asking about belief in God. However, a 1944 Gallup survey, the earliest in their historical series for this question, found 96 percent of Americans stating a belief in God. See Gallup Historical Trends, "Religion," accessed December 30, 2022, www.gallup.com.

11 Leuba, *The Belief in God and Immortality*, 254.

12 James H. Leuba, "Religious Beliefs of American Scientists" *Harper's Magazine* 169 (1934): 291–300.

13 Edward J. Larson and Larry Witham, "Scientists Are Still Keeping the Faith," *Nature* 386 (1996): 435–36. Emphasis added.

14 Edward J. Larson and Larry Witham, "Leading Scientists Still Reject God," *Nature* 394 (1998): 313–14.

15 For a discussion of some other limitations, see C. Mackenzie Brown, "The Conflict between Religion and Science in Light of the Patterns of Religious Belief among Scientists," *Zygon* 38, no. 3 (2003): 603–32.

16 Leuba actually used two versions of this question. In the other version, the first choice was, "I believe in a God in intellectual and affective communication with man, I mean a God to whom one may pray in the expectation of receiving an answer. By 'answer,' I do not mean the subjective, psychological effect of prayer." The second choice was worded the same. The third choice was worded, "I am an agnostic."

17 Elaine Howard Ecklund, *Science vs. Religion: What Scientists Really Think* (New York: Oxford University Press, 2010).

18 Another 30 percent said that they "do not know if there is a God, and there is no way to find out."

19 American Chemical Society, *ACS Graduate Student Survey*, 2013, accessed November, 1, 2019, www.acs.org.

20 Rodney Stark, "On the Incompatibility of Religion and Science: A Survey of American Graduate Students," *Journal for the Scientific Study of Religion* 3, no. 1 (1963): 3–20.

21 Philip Schwadel, "Does Higher Education Cause Religious Decline? A Longitudinal Analysis of the Within- and Between-Person Effects of Higher Education on Religiosity," *Sociological Quarterly* 57, no. 4 (2016): 759–86.

22 This percentage is based on those age 22 to 35 with at least a bachelor's degree, who identified as "none" in response to the religious identity question (RELIG) on the 2018 General Social Survey.

23 The quotation from the book is: "Isn't it enough to see that a garden is beautiful without having to believe that there are fairies at the bottom of it too?" Douglas Adams, *The Hitchhiker's Guide to the Galaxy* (New York: Pocket Books, 1980), 118.

24 It is important to acknowledge that there is significant variation in the types of atheism both in the general public and among scientists. See, for instance, Elaine Howard Ecklund and David R. Johnson, *Varieties of Atheism in Science* (New York: Oxford University Press, 2021).

25 Interview 128 (male, physics, atheist), conducted on May 16, 2019.

26 Interview 160 (male, chemistry, agnostic), conducted on June 27, 2019.

27 While the atheist and agnostic group are closer to each other than the other categories, there are some slight differences between the two. For instance, the agnostic group is a little more likely to still identify with a religion (18% identify with some religion, as compared to 9% for atheists) and somewhat more likely to attend religious services, at least sporadically (74% of atheists never attend, as compared to 59% of agnostics).

28 The survey data, for instance, finds that the correlation between attendance and belief in God is .61. While strong, this is slightly weaker than the correlation between belief in God and self-perceived religiosity at .74.

29 Interview 116 (male, biology, Christian), conducted on April 25, 2019.

30 Interview 107 (male, physics, Christian), conducted on April 3, 2019.

31 This question is strongly correlated with other measures, as its correlation with attendance (.74) and belief in God (also .74) is fairly strong.

32 Interview 109 (male, sociology, Jewish), conducted on May 2, 2019.

33 Interview 157 (female, psychology, Hindu), conducted on June 26, 2019.

34 Leuba, *The Belief in God and Immortality*, 279.

35 Edward C. Lehman Jr. and Donald W. Shriver Jr., "Academic Discipline as Predictive of Faculty Religiosity," *Social Forces* 47, no. 2 (1968): 171–82.

36 Robert Wuthnow, "Science and the Sacred," in *The Sacred in a Secular Age*, edited by Phillip E. Hammond, 187–203 (Berkeley: University of California Press, 1985).

37 Neil Gross and Solon Simmons, "The Religiosity of American College and University Professors," *Sociology of Religion* 70, no. 2 (2009): 101–29.

38 Elaine Howard Ecklund and Christopher P. Scheitle, "Religion among Academic Scientists: Distinctions, Disciplines, and Demographics," *Social Problems* 54, no. 2 (2007): 289–307.

39 Leuba, *The Belief in God and Immortality*, 285–86.

40 Some of Leuba's contemporaries did challenge his interpretation on this point. One writer argued that the weaker religiosity of the more elite scientists might be due to their narrow intellectual obsession with science, which leads to the exclusion of other life pursuits, including religion. Writing more recently, Brown, in "The Conflict between Religion and Science in Light of the Patterns of Religious Belief among Scientists," rejects this argument based on the idea that education tends to "broaden a student's horizons in various areas of arts, humanities, and sciences" rather than narrow them. For my part, I do not see these arguments as mutually exclusive. It may be true that education increases knowledge of, say, world religions. But the pursuit of high levels of science (or other professions, for that matter) might reduce one's time and interest in pursuing those religions and restrict one's source of identity to a narrower social sphere.

41 Granted, my survey only covered the top sixty programs in each discipline, so it is possible that there may differences even further down the rankings.

42 Timothy S. Rich, "Publishing as a Graduate Student: A Quick and (Hopefully) Painless Guide to Establishing Yourself as a Scholar," *PS: Political Science & Politics* 46, no. 2 (2013): 376–79; John Robert Warren, "How Much Do You Have to Publish to Get a Job in a Top Sociology Department. Or to Get Tenure? Trends over a Generation," *Sociological Science* 6, no. 1 (2019): 172–96.

43 These are predicted counts produced from a negative binominal regression model predicting the number of publications while adjusting for student discipline, year in program, and ranking tier of program.

44 Darren E. Sherkat, *Changing Faith: The Dynamics and Consequences of Americans' Shifting Religious Identities* (New York: New York University Press, 2014); Christopher P. Scheitle, Katie E. Corcoran, and Caitlin Halligan, "The Rise of the Nones and the Changing Relationships Between Identity, Belief, and Behavior," *Journal of Contemporary Religion* 33, no. 3 (2018): 567–79.

45 Interview 144 (male, sociology atheist), conducted on June 6, 2019.

CHAPTER 2. VIEWS ON THE RELIGION-SCIENCE RELATIONSHIP

1 This and the subsequent quotations attributed to Jessica are from Interview 137 (female, chemistry, nonreligious), conducted on May 30, 2019.

2 This and the subsequent quotations attributed to Arjun are from Interview 140 (male, physics, Hindu), conducted on May 30, 2019.

3 Ian G. Barbour, *Religion and Science: Historical and Contemporary Issues* (New York: HarperCollins, 1997).

4 David Van Biema, "God vs. Science," *Time*, November 5, 2006, www.time.com.

5 Interview 119 (female, biology, nonreligious), conducted on May 3, 2019.

6 Stephen Jay Gould, "Nonoverlapping Magisteria," *Natural History* 106, no. 2 (1997): 16–22.

7 Note that Barbour distinguishes between collaboration thinkers who take a "dialogue" approach and those that take an "integration" approach.

8 Greg Cootsona, "When Science Comes to Church," *Christianity Today*, March 5, 2014, www.christianitytoday.com.

9 Lawrence M. Principe, "The Warfare Thesis," in *The Warfare Between Science and Religion: The Idea that Wouldn't Die*, edited by Jeff Hardin, Ronald L. Numbers, and Ronald A. Binzley, 6–26 (Baltimore: Johns Hopkins University Press, 2018).

10 Elizabeth Dias, "What You Missed While Not Watching the Bill Nye and Ken Ham Creation Debate," *Time*, February 5, 2014, www.time.com.

11 Elaine Howard Ecklund and Christopher P. Scheitle, *Religion vs. Science: What Religious People Really Think* (New York: Oxford University Press, 2018), 17. The question we asked was, "For me personally, my understanding of science and religion can be described as a relationship of . . . (1) Conflict – I consider myself on the side of religion (2) Conflict – I consider myself on the side of science (3) Independence – They refer to different aspects of reality (4) Collaboration – Each can be used to support the other."

12 See, for instance, Joseph O. Baker, "Public Perceptions of Incompatibility between 'Science and Religion,'" *Public Understanding of Science* 21, no. 3 (2012): 340–53.

13 Joseph O. Baker, "Public Perceptions of Incompatibility between 'Science and Religion,'" *Public Understanding of Science* 21, no. 3 (2012): 340–53.

14 Bruce Hunsberger and Bob Altemeyer, *Atheists: A Groundbreaking Study of America's Nonbelievers* (Amherst, NY: Prometheus Books, 2006); Stephen LeDrew, "Reply: Toward a Critical Sociology of Atheism: Identity, Politics, Ideology," *Sociology of Religion* 74, no. 4 (2013): 464–70; Jesse M. Smith, "Becoming an Atheist in America: Constructing Identity and Meaning from the Rejection of Theism," *Sociology of Religion* 72, no. 2 (2011): 215–37.

15 Interview 102 (male, biology, Christian), conducted on March 21, 2019.

16 Interview 151 (male, chemistry, agnostic), conducted on June 13, 2019.

17 See, for instance, Joseph O. Baker, "Public Perceptions of Incompatibility between 'Science and Religion,'" *Public Understanding of Science* 21, no. 3 (2012): 340–53. Note, though, that even among literalists these surveys show that it is a minority of individuals who see conflict between science and religion.

18 This is a core argument of an earlier book I wrote with Ecklund, *Religion vs. Science*.

19 D. Michael. Lindsay, *Faith in the Halls of Power: How Evangelicals Joined the American Elite* (New York: Oxford University Press, 2007); Geoffrey Layman, "Religion and Political Behavior in the United States: The Impact of Beliefs, Affiliations, and Commitment from 1980 to 1994," *Public Opinion Quarterly* 61, no. 2 (1997): 288–316; Clem Brooks and Jeff Manza, "A Great Divide? Religion and

Political Change in U.S. National Elections, 1972–2000," *Sociological Quarterly* 45, no. 3 (2004): 421–50.

20 Michael Hout and Claude S. Fischer, "Explaining Why More Americans Have No Religious Preference: Political Backlash and Generational Succession, 1987–2012," *Sociological Science* 1, no. 1 (2014): 423–47.

21 Sheila S. Jasanoff, "Contested Boundaries in Policy-Relevant Science," *Social Studies of Science* 17 (1987): 195–230.

22 Union of Concerned Scientists, "History," accessed December 30, 2022, www .ucsusa.org/about/history.

23 Gordon Gauchat, "Politicization of Science in the Public Sphere: A Study of Public Trust in the United States, 1974 to 2010," *American Sociological Review* 77, no. 2 (2012): 167–87; Timothy L. O'Brien and Shiri Noy, "Political Identity and Confidence in Science and Religion in the United States," *Sociology of Religion* 81, no. 4 (2020): 439–61.

24 John H. Evans, "The Growing Social and Moral Conflict between Conservative Protestantism and Science," *Journal for the Scientific Study of Religion* 52, no. 2 (2013): 368–85.

25 Interview 117 (male, physics, Christian), conducted on May 14, 2019.

26 Interview 119 (female, biology, nonreligious), conducted on May 3, 2019.

27 Interview 102 (male, biology, Christian), conducted on March 21, 2019.

28 Interview 127 (female, psychology, agnostic), conducted on May 10, 2019.

29 Interview 145 (female, chemistry, Muslim), conducted on June 6, 2019.

30 PBS, "An Interview with Francis Collins," *The Question of God*, 2004, www.pbs.org.

31 Interview 155 (male, psychology, Christian), conducted on June 26, 2019.

32 Interview 102 (male, biology, Christian), conducted on March 21, 2019.

33 Interview 135 (female, psychology, Christian), conducted on May 22, 2019.

34 Interview 110 (male, physics, Muslim), conducted on April 11, 2019.

35 David DeSteno, "What Science Can Learn from Religion," *New York Times*, February 1, 2019, www.nytimes.com.

36 Interview 129 (male, sociology, Jewish), conducted on May 20, 2019.

37 Interview 105 (male, chemistry, Christian), conducted on March 27, 2019.

38 Interview 146 (female, biology, Mormon), conducted on June 10, 2019.

39 Interview 145 (female, chemistry, Muslim), conducted on June 6, 2019.

40 Interview 131 (male, physics, Christian), conducted on May 17, 2019.

41 Interview 117 (male, physics, Christian), conducted on May 14, 2019.

42 Interview 121 (male, chemistry, Mormon), conducted on May 2, 2019.

43 Interview 163 (male, chemistry, atheist), conducted on June 28, 2019.

44 Interview 127 (female, psychology, agnostic), conducted on May 10, 2019.

CHAPTER 3. STIGMA AND HOSTILITY

1 This and all subsequent quotations attributed to Emily are from Interview 136 (female, biology, Christian), conducted on May 28, 2019.

2 Jeffrey M. Poirier, Courtney Tanenbaum, Charles Storey, Rita Kirshstein, and Carlos Rodriguez, *The Road to the STEM Professoriate for Underrepresented Minorities: A Review of the Literature* (Washington, DC: American Institutes for Research, 2009); Heidi Blackburn, "The Status of Women in STEM in Higher Education: A Review of the Literature 2007–2017," *Science & Technology Libraries* 36, no. 3 (2017): 235–73.

3 Laura Beth Kelly, "An Analysis of Award-winning Science Trade Books for Children: Who Are the Scientists, and What is Science?" *Journal of Research in Science Teaching* 55, no. 8 (2018): 1188–1210.

4 Catherine Good, Aneeta Rattan, and Carol S. Dweck. "Why Do Women Opt Out? Sense of Belonging and Women's Representation in Mathematics," *Journal of Personality and Social Psychology* 102, no. 4 (2012): 700–17.

5 Louise Archer, Jennifer Dewitt, and Jonathan Osborne, "Is Science for Us? Black Students' and Parents' Views of Science and Science Careers," *Science Education.* 99, no. 2 (2015): 199–237.

6 Jennifer L. Glass, Sharon Sassler, Yael Levitte, and Katherine M. Michelmore. "What's So Special about STEM? A Comparison of Women's Retention in STEM and Professional Occupations," *Social Forces.* 92, no. 2 (2013): 723–56.

7 In comparison, only 19 percent of men reported such an experience.

8 In comparison, only 14 percent of white students reported such an experience.

9 There is a parallel here to what sexuality scholars have observed in "assumed heterosexuality" in a variety of social settings. That is, it is typically assumed that everyone is heterosexual unless that assumption is explicitly challenged by someone in the setting. See, for example: Andrea Daley, "Lesbian Health and the Assumption of Heterosexuality: An Organizational Perspective," *Canadian Journal of Community Mental Health* 22, no. 2 (2003): 105–21; Annie Dignan, "Outdoor Education and the Reinforcement of Heterosexuality," *Journal of Outdoor and Environmental Education* 6, no. 2 (2002): 77–80; Damien W. Riggs, "Reassessing the Foster-Care System: Examining the Impact of Heterosexism on Lesbian and Gay Applicants," *Hypatia* 22, no. 1 (2007): 132–48.

10 Penny Edgell, Joseph Gerteis, and Douglas Hartmann, "Atheists as 'Other': Moral Boundaries and Cultural Membership in American Society," *American Sociological Review* 71, no. 2 (2006): 211–34.

11 Interview 163 (male, chemistry, atheist), conducted on June 28, 2019.

12 Interview 120 (female, biology, nonreligious), conducted on May 16, 2019.

13 Interview 128 (male, physics, atheist), conducted on May 16, 2019.

14 Interview 120 (female, biology, nonreligious), conducted on May 16, 2019.

15 Interview 107 (male, physics, Christian), conducted on April 3, 2019.

16 Interview 141 (female, psychology, Christian), conducted on May 23, 2019.

17 Interview 161 (male, physics, agnostic), conducted on June 27, 2019.

18 Interview 118 (male, physics, Christian), conducted on April 30, 2019.

19 Interview 116 (male, biology, Christian), conducted on April 25, 2019.

20 Interview 141 (female, psychology, Christian), conducted on May 23, 2019.

21 Interview 131 (male, physics, Christian), conducted on May 17, 2019.

22 Interview 153 (female, chemistry, Christian), conducted on June 18, 2019.

23 Interview 133 (male, chemistry, Jewish), conducted on May 21, 2019.

24 Interview 116 (male, biology, Christian), conducted on April 25, 2019.

25 Joseph H. Hammer, Ryan T. Cragun, Karen Hwang, and Jesse M. Smith, "Forms, Frequency, and Correlates of Perceived Anti-Atheist Discrimination," *Secularism and Nonreligion*, 1 (2012): 43–67; Ryan T. Cragun, Barry Kosmin, Ariela Keysar, Joseph H. Hammer, and Michael Nielsen, "On the Receiving End: Discrimination toward the Non-Religious in the United States," *Journal of Contemporary Religion* 27, no. 1 (2012): 105–27; Bradley R. E. Wright, Michael Wallace, John Bailey, and Allen Hyde, "Religious Affiliation and Hiring Discrimination in New England: A Field Experiment," *Research in Social Stratification and Mobility* 34 (2013): 111–26.

26 Fourteen percent of women say that, due to gender, they are treated with less respect "a few times a year," 6 percent say this happens "a few times a month," and 2 percent say this happens "at least once a week or more." Fifteen percent of black students say that, due to race, they are treated with less respect "a few times a year," 6 percent say this happens "a few times a month," and 11 percent say this happens "at least once a week or more."

27 Of course, this burden should not fall entirely on religious individuals. The nonreligious also have a role in challenging behavior that is creating a hostile climate for others.

28 Elaine Howard Ecklund, *Science vs. Religion: What Scientists Really Think* (New York: Oxford University Press, 2010), 43. Interestingly, in Leuba's study of religion among scientists (*The Belief in God and Immortality*, 272–73), published almost one hundred years earlier, he argued that it was nonreligious scientists who were more likely to conceal their identities. He observed that scientists who said they were believers on his survey were more likely to have voluntarily provided a signature with their survey response than those who expressed disbelief.

29 Interview 116 (male, biology, Christian), conducted on April 25, 2019.

30 Interview 122 (female, sociology, Christian), conducted on May 14, 2019.

31 Kristin P. Beals, Letitia Anne Peplau, and Shelly L. Gable, "Stigma Management and Well-Being: The Role of Perceived Social Support, Emotional Processing, and Suppression," *Personality and Social Psychology Bulletin* 35, no. 7 (2009): 867–79; Juan M. Madera, Eden B. King, and Michelle R. Hebl, "Bringing Social Identity to Work: The Influence of Manifestation and Suppression on Perceived Discrimination, Job Satisfaction, and Turnover Intentions," *Cultural Diversity and Ethnic Minority Psychology* 18, no. 2 (2012): 165–70; Anna-Kaisa Newheiser and Manuela Barreto, "Hidden Costs of Hiding Stigma: Ironic Interpersonal Consequences of Concealing a Stigmatized Identity in Social Interactions," *Journal of Experimental Social Psychology* 52 (2014): 58–70.

32 Interview 103 (female, sociology, Christian), conducted on March 26, 2019.

33 Interview 116 (male, biology, Christian), conducted on April 25, 2019.

34 Interview 133 (male, chemistry, Jewish), conducted on May 21, 2019.

35 Erving Goffman, *Stigma: Notes on the Management of Spoiled Identity* (New York: Simon & Schuster, 1963).

36 Interview 131 (male, physics, Christian), conducted on May 17, 2019.

37 Interview 147 (female, chemistry, Christian), conducted on June 12, 2019.

38 American Psychological Association, "Think Again: Men and Women Share Cognitive Skills," 2014, www.apa.org.

39 Mara Cadinu, Anne Maass, Alessandra Rosabianca, and Jeff Kiesner, "Why Do Women Underperform under Stereotype Threat? Evidence for the Role of Negative Thinking," *Psychological Science* 16, no. 7 (2005): 572–78; Ilan Dar-Nimrod and Steven J. Heine, "Exposure to Scientific Theories Affects Women's Math Performance," *Science* 314 (2006): 435; Maya A. Beasley and Mary J. Fischer, "Why They Leave: The Impact of Stereotype Threat on the Attrition of Women and Minorities from Science, Math and Engineering Majors," *Social Psychology of Education* 15, no. 4 (2012): 427–48.

40 Rios, Kimberly, Zhen Hadassah Cheng, Rebecca R. Totton, and Azim F. Shariff, "Negative Stereotypes Cause Christians to Underperform in and Disidentify with Science," *Social Psychological and Personality Science* 6, no. 8 (2015): 959–67.

41 Interview 146 (female, biology, Mormon), conducted on June 10, 2019.

42 Interview 105 (male, chemistry, Christian), conducted on March 27, 2019.

43 Interview 145 (female, chemistry, Muslim), conducted on June 6, 2019.

CHAPTER 4. ADVISORS AND PEERS

1 This and all subsequent quotations attributed to Catherine are from Interview 135 (female, psychology, Christian), conducted on May 30, 2019.

2 Interview 132 (female, psychology, Christian), conducted on May 21, 2019.

3 Interview 125 (female, chemistry, Christian), conducted on May 17, 2019.

4 Interview 130 (male, physics, Christian), conducted on May 13, 2019.

5 Interview 160 (male, chemistry, agnostic), conducted on June 27, 2019.

6 Daniel Fuerstman and Stephan Lavertu, "The Academic Hiring Process: A Survey of Department Chairs," *PS: Political Science & Politics* 38, no. 4 (2005): 731–36; Lauren A. Rivera, "When Two Bodies Are (Not) a Problem: Gender and Relationship Status Discrimination in Academic Hiring," *American Sociological Review* 82, no. 6 (2017): 1111–38.

7 Corinne A. Moss-Racusin, John F. Dovidio, Victoria L. Brescoll, Mark J. Graham, and Jo Handelsman, "Science Faculty's Subtle Gender Biases Favor Male Students," *Proceedings of the National Academy of Sciences* 109, no. 41 (2012): 16474–79.

8 Gaule and Piacentini, for instance, argue that the "lower availability of same-gender advisors for female students" (p. 805) perpetuates the lack of female representation in science. Patrick Gaule and Mario Piacentini, "An Advisor Like

Me? Advisor Gender and Post-Graduate Careers in Science," *Research Policy* 47, no. 4 (2018): 805–13.

9   Elyse Goldstein, "Effect of Same-Sex and Cross-Sex Role Models on the Subsequent Academic Productivity of Scholars," *American Psychologist* 34, no. 5 (1979): 407–10; Christiana Hilmer and Michael Hilmer, "Women Helping Women, Men Helping Women? Same-Gender Mentoring, Initial Job Placements, and Early Career Publishing Success for Economics PhDs," *American Economic Review* 97, no. 2 (2007): 422–26; Stacy Blake-Beard, Melissa L. Bayne, Faye J. Crosby, and Carol B. Muller, "Matching by Race and Gender in Mentoring Relationships: Keeping Our Eyes on the Prize," *Journal of Social Issues* 67, no. 3 (2011): 622–43; Michele Pezzoni, Jacques Mairesse, Paula Stephan, and Julia Lane, "Gender and the Publication Output of Graduate Students: A Case Study," *PLoS One* 11, no. 1 (2016): e0145146.

10 Blake-Beard et al., "Matching by Race and Gender in Mentoring Relationships."

11 Paul R. Hernandez, Mica Estrada, Anna Woodcock, and P. Wesley Schultz, "Protégé Perceptions of High Mentorship Quality Depend on Shared Values More Than on Demographic Match," *Journal of Experimental Education* 85, no. 3 (2017): 450–68.

12 One reason relates to the salience of an identity to a student. Research has shown that individuals belonging to a group that is in the numerical minority or is otherwise marginalized tend to place greater salience on that identity than individuals who belong to the dominant group. Individuals who belong to a religious group that is in the minority in a particular geographic context, for example, will tend to place more emphasis on their religious identity and increase their religious activities when compared to individuals in the same religious group in a geographic context where that group represents the majority of the population. Similarly, in the United States, racial or ethnical minorities tend to place more emphasis on their racial or ethnic identity than White or European Americans. See Rodney Stark and Roger Finke, "Religions in Context: The Response of Non-Mormon Faiths in Utah," *Review of Religious Research* 45, no. 3 (2004): 293–98; Stella Ting-Toomey, Kimberlie K. Yee-Jung, Robin B. Shapiro, Wintilo Garcia, Trina J. Wright, and John G. Oetzel, "Ethnic/Cultural Identity Salience and Conflict Styles in Four US Ethnic Groups," *International Journal of Intercultural Relations* 24, no. 1 (2000): 47–81; Sylvia Hurtado, Adriana Ruiz Alvarado, and Chelsea Guillermo-Wann, "Thinking about Race: The Salience of Racial Identity at Two-and Four-year Colleges and the Climate for Diversity," *Journal of Higher Education* 86, no. 1 (2015): 127–55.

13 The findings are the same for other religious groups. For instance, 92.8 percent of Jewish students and 100 percent of Muslim, Hindu, Buddhist, Sikh students say their advisors' religion is not important to them at all.

14 Interview 114 (female, psychology, Mormon), conducted on April 16, 2019.

15 Interview 122 (female, sociology, Christian), conducted on May 14, 2019.

16 Interview 157, (female, psychology, Hindu), conducted on June 26, 2019.

17 Interview 136 (female, biology, Christian), conducted on May 28, 2019.

18 Interview 116 (male, biology, Christian), conducted on April 25, 2019.

19 Interview 131 (male, physics, Christian), conducted on May 17, 2019.

20 Interview 129 (male, sociology, Jewish), conducted on May 20, 2019.

21 Patricia Adler and Peter Adler, "The Identity Career of the Graduate Student: Professional Socialization to Academic Sociology," *American Sociologist* 36, no. 2 (2005): 11–27; Matthew W. Kemp, Timothy J. Molloy, Marina Pajic, and Elaine Chapman, "Peer Relationships and the Biomedical Doctorate: A Key Component of the Contemporary Learning Environment," *Journal of Higher Education Policy and Management* 35, no. 4 (2013): 370–85; Susan Furr and Kathleen Brown-Rice, "Psychology Doctoral Students' Perceptions of Peers' Problems of Professional Competency," *Training and Education in Professional Psychology* 12, no. 2 (2018): 118–24.

22 Interview 157 (female, psychology, Hindu), conducted on June 26, 2019.

23 Timothy M. Osberg, Katherine Billingsley, Meredith Eggert, and Maribeth Insana, "From Animal House to Old School: A Multiple Mediation Analysis of the Association between College Drinking Movie Exposure and Freshman Drinking and Its Consequences," *Addictive Behaviors* 37, no. 8 (2012): 922–30.

24 Crystal L. Park, "Positive and Negative Consequences of Alcohol Consumption in College Students," *Addictive Behaviors* 29, no. 2 (2004): 311–21.

25 Lizabeth A. Crawford and Katherine B. Novak, "Alcohol Abuse as a Rite of Passage: The Effect of Beliefs about Alcohol and the College Experience on Undergraduates' Drinking Behaviors," *Journal of Drug Education* 36, no. 3 (2006): 193–212; Timothy M. Osberg, Lindsay Atkins, Laura Buchholz, Victoria Shirshova, Andrew Swiantek, Jessica Whitley, Sabrina Hartman, and Natasha Oquendo, "Development and Validation of the College Life Alcohol Salience Scale: A Measure of Beliefs about the Role of Alcohol in College Life," *Psychology of Addictive Behaviors* 24, no. 1 (2010): 1–12.

26 E. L. Meszaros, "Disentangling Grad School and Alcohol Culture," *Brown Daily Herald*, September 4, 2019, browndailyherald.com.

27 Hannah K. Allen, Angelica L. Barrall, Kenneth H. Beck, Kathryn B. Vincent, and Amelia M. Arria, "Situational Context and Motives of Alcohol Use among Graduate Student Drinkers," *Addictive Behaviors* 104, article 106267 (2020): 1–7.

28 Gayle M. Wells, "The Effect of Religiosity and Campus Alcohol Culture on Collegiate Alcohol Consumption," *Journal of American College Health* 58, no. 4 (2010): 295–304; Julie A. Patock-Peckham, Geoffrey T. Hutchinson, Jeewon Cheong, and Craig T. Nagoshi, "Effect of Religion and Religiosity on Alcohol Use in a College Student Sample," *Drug and Alcohol Dependence* 49, no. 2 (1998): 81–88; Cochran, John K., Leonard Beeghley, and E. Wilbur Bock, "Religiosity and Alcohol Behavior: An Exploration of Reference Group Theory," *Sociological Forum* 3, no. 2 (1988): 256–76.

29 My research isn't the only evidence of these concerns. For instance, a few years ago a student's letter to an advice column serving Christian women in academia operated by the organization InterVarsity asked, "I'm concerned that my avoidance of alcohol may earn me a reputation for being anti-social . . . Do you have any suggestions for how best to navigate the drinking culture of academia as a teetotaler, while also connecting with friends?" "Dear Mentor: Alcohol in Grad School?" *The Well*, February 25, 2016, thewell.intervarsity.org.

30 Interview 121 (male, chemistry, Mormon), conducted on May 2, 2019.

31 Interview 110 (male, physics, Muslim), conducted on April 11, 2019.

32 Interview 165 (female, chemistry, Mormon), conducted on June 28, 2019.

33 Interview 114 (female, psychology, Mormon), conducted on April 16, 2019.

34 Interview 159 (female, physics, Christian), conducted on June 27, 2019.

35 Vicki L. Baker and Meghan J. Pifer, "The Role of Relationships in the Transition from Doctoral Student to Independent Scholar," *Studies in Continuing Education* 33, no. 1 (2011): 5–17.

36 Interview 146 (female, biology, Mormon), conducted on June 10, 2019.

37 Interview 150 (male, chemistry, Christian), conducted on June 13, 2019.

38 Interview 135 (female, psychology, Christian), conducted on May 30, 2019.

39 Interview 131 (male, physics, Christian), conducted on May 17, 2019.

40 Interview 147 (female, chemistry, Christian), conducted on June 12, 2019.

41 Marian Jazvac-Martek, Shuhua Chen, and Lynn McAlpine, "Tracking the Doctoral Student Experience over Time: Cultivating Agency in Diverse Spaces," in *Doctoral Education: Research-Based Strategies for Doctoral Students, Supervisors and Administrators*, edited by Lynn McAlpine and Cheryl Amundsen, 17–36 (Dordrecht, Netherlands: Springer, 2011); Mark S. Granovetter, "The Strength of Weak Ties," *American Journal of Sociology* 78, no. 6 (1973): 1360–80.

42 Vicki L. Baker and Lisa R. Lattuca, "Developmental Networks and Learning: Toward an Interdisciplinary Perspective on Identity Development during Doctoral Study," *Studies in Higher Education* 35, no. 7 (2010): 807–27.

43 Vicki L. Sweitzer, "Networking to Develop a Professional Identity: A Look at the First-Semester Experience of Doctoral Students in Business," *New Directions for Teaching and Learning* 113, no. 1 (2008): 43–56.

CHAPTER 5. IDENTITY AND PURPOSE

1 This and all subsequent quotations attributed to Eric are from Interview 130 (male, physics, Christian), conducted on May 13, 2019.

2 Interview 150 (male, chemistry, Christian), conducted on June 13, 2019.

3 Interview 146 (female, biology, Mormon), conducted on June 10, 2019.

4 Interview 103 (female, sociology, Christian), conducted on March 26, 2019.

5 Interview 132 (female, psychology, Christian), conducted on May 21, 2019.

6 Kendall Powell, "Work–Life Balance: Break or Burn Out" *Nature* 545 (2017): 375–77; "Encouraging Science Outreach," *Nature Neuroscience*. 12, no. 6 (2009):

665; Elaine Howard Ecklund, Sarah A. James, and Anne E. Lincoln, "How Academic Biologists and Physicists View Science Outreach," *PloS One* 7, no. 5 (2012): e36240.

7 Elaine Howard Ecklund and Elizabeth Long, "Scientists and Spirituality," *Sociology of Religion* 72, no. 3 (2011): 253–74.

8 Interview 103 (female, sociology, Christian), conducted on March 26, 2019.

9 Interview 107 (male, physics, Christian), conducted on April 3, 2019.

10 Interview 156 (female, psychology, nonreligious), conducted on June 26, 2019.

11 Interview 129 (male, sociology, Jewish), conducted on May 20, 2019.

12 Matthew R. Bennett and Christopher J. Einolf, "Religion, Altruism, and Helping Strangers: A Multilevel Analysis of 126 Countries," *Journal for the Scientific Study of Religion* 56, no. 2 (2017): 323–41; Christopher J. Einolf, "The Link between Religion and Helping Others: The Role of Values, Ideas, and Language," *Sociology of Religion* 72, no. 4 (2011): 435–55. Note that some research does suggest that the content or specifics of the religious beliefs an individual holds can have varying effects on outcomes like altruism. See, for instance, Lisa Hoffmann, Matthias Basedau, Simone Gobien, and Sebastian Prediger, "Universal Love or One True Religion? Experimental Evidence of the Ambivalent Effect of Religious Ideas on Altruism and Discrimination," *American Journal of Political Science* 64, no. 3 (2020): 603–20.

13 The question is more whether religion may provide, on average, a more powerful and consistent effect than other ethical or moral motivators, or whether religion may be a particularly prominent motivator given its larger presence. This issue is found in most research looking at the effects of religion on pro-social outcomes. In discussing the influence of religious "moral directives" on positive youth outcomes, the sociologist Christian Smith observes:

> Of course, religions are not the only source of such moral directives and orders . . . American youth (as do all modern people) therefore find themselves living within and between multiple moral orders among which they have to negotiate, balance, compromise, and choose. Religion represents one of many potential normative orders claiming youth's allegiance and adherence. While other nonreligious moral orders . . . may promote virtues and values similar to those of a religious moral order, clearly not all do.

Christian Smith, "Theorizing Religious Effects among American Adolescents," *Journal for the Scientific Study of Religion* 42, no. 1 (2003): 17–30.

14 Interview 101 (female, sociology, not religious), conducted on March 21, 2019.

15 Interview 135 (female, psychology, Christian), conducted on May 30, 2019.

16 Elaine Howard Ecklund, *Why Science and Faith Need Each Other: Eight Shared Values that Move Us Beyond Fear* (Grand Rapids, MI: Brazos Press, 2020), 85–89.

17 Interview 135 (female, psychology, Christian), conducted on May 30, 2019.

18 Interview 116 (male, biology, Christian), conducted on April 25, 2019.

19 Max Weber, *The Protestant Ethic and the Spirit of Capitalism*, translated and edited by Stephen Kalberg (New York: Oxford University Press, 2011 [1920]).

20 See, for instance, Selçuk Uygur, Laura J. Spence, Ruth Simpson, and Fahri Karakas, "Work Ethic, Religion and Moral Energy: The Case of Turkish SME Owner-Managers," *International Journal of Human Resource Management* 28, no. 8 (2017): 1212–35; Eberhard Feess, Helge Mueller, and Sabrina G. Ruhnau, "The Impact of Religion and the Degree of Religiosity on Work Ethic: A Multilevel Analysis," *Kyklos* 67, no. 4 (2014): 506–34.

21 Interview 140 (male, physics, Hindu), conducted on May 30, 2019.

22 This leads to no shortage of advice columns concerning time management for graduate students. For instance: Amy Novotney, "Where Do the Hours Go?" *gradPSYCH Magazine* 3 (2013): 26.

23 Interview 164 (male, physics, agnostic), conducted on June 28, 2019.

24 Interview 138 (male, biology, pagan), conducted on May 28, 2019.

25 Interview 150 (male, chemistry, Christian), conducted on June 13, 2019.

26 Luca Rinaldi, "Rescuing My Time from Science," *Science* 354, no. 6319 (2016): 1666.

27 Interview 111 (male, sociology, Jewish), conducted on April 16, 2019.

28 Interview 138 (male, biology, pagan), conducted on May 28, 2019.

CHAPTER 6. FAMILY AND CAREER

1 Interview 139 (female, sociology, Christian), conducted on May 23, 2019.

2 Elaine Ecklund and Anne E. Lincoln, *Failing Families, Failing Science: Work-family Conflict in Academic Science* (New York: New York University Press, 2016); Mary Frank Fox, Carolyn Fonseca, and Jinghui Bao, "Work and Family Conflict in Academic Science: Patterns and Predictors among Women and Men in Research Universities," *Social Studies of Science* 41, no. 5 (2011): 715–35.

3 See, for instance: Vanessa A. Jean, Stephanie C. Payne, and Rebecca J. Thompson, "Women in STEM: Family-Related Challenges and Initiatives," in *Gender and the Work-Family Experience*, edited by Maura J. Mills, 291–311 (Cham, Switzerland: Springer, 2015); Erica S. Weisgram and Amanda B. Diekman, "Making STEM 'Family Friendly': The Impact of Perceiving Science Careers as Family-Compatible," *Social Sciences* 6, no. 2 (2017): 1–19. Note, however, that research also shows that many men in science struggle with work–family tensions, and this has likely increased over time as cultural norms have shifted and increasing numbers of male scientists have partners who also work full-time. See Sarah Damaske, Elaine Howard Ecklund, Anne E. Lincoln, and Virginia J. White, "Male Scientists' Competing Devotions to Work and Family: Changing Norms in a Male-Dominated Profession," *Work and Occupations* 41, no. 4 (2014): 477–507.

4 This idealized image is sometimes presented in popular culture, such as the TV show *The Big Bang Theory*. The primary figure in the show, the physicist Sheldon Cooper, maintains his eyes on winning the Nobel Prize and states at one point

that "Science demands nothing less than the fervent and unconditional dedication of our entire lives." Chuck Lorre, Bill Prady, Tim Doyle, Richard Rosenstock, and Stephen Engel, "The Cooper-Nowitzki Theorem," season 2, episode 6 of *The Big Bang Theory*, CBS, original air date November 3, 2008.

5 Walter Isaacson, *Einstein: His Life and Universe* (London: Simon & Schuster, 2007), 161.

6 National Center for Science and Engineering Statistics, "Median Years to Doctorate, by Major Field of Study: Selected Years, 1994–2019," *Survey of Earned Doctorates*, 2019, https://ncses.nsf.gov/pubs/nsf21308/data-tables.

7 For readers who may not be familiar with academia, a postdoctoral position ("postdoc") is a fuzzy middle state of not quite being a graduate student while not quite being a professor. It has been referred to by some as the postdoc "purgatory." These positions are often one- or two-year positions in which the postdoc works under the supervision of a professor. Sam Jaffe and Paula Park, "Postdocs: Pawing Out of Purgatory," *The Scientist* 17, no. 6 (2003): 46; Kendall Powell, "The Future of the Postdoc," *Nature* 520, no. 7546 (2015): 144–47.

8 Interview 131 (male, physics, Christian), conducted on May 17, 2019.

9 Elaine Howard Ecklund and Anne E. Lincoln, "Scientists Want More Children," *PLOS ONE* 6, no. 8 (2011): 1–4.

10 Interview 113 (female, psychology, pagan), conducted on April 30, 2019.

11 Interview 108 (female, psychology, Hindu), conducted on April 3, 2019.

12 Interview 147 (female, chemistry, Christian), conducted on June 12, 2019.

13 Scott Jaschik, "Making Grad School 'Family-Friendly,'" *Inside Higher Ed*, April 4, 2007, www.insidehighered.com; Kristen W. Springer, Brenda K. Parker, and Catherine Leviten-Reid, "Making Space for Graduate Student Parents: Practice and Politics," *Journal of Family Issues* 30, no. 4 (2009): 435–57.

14 See Xianwen Wang, Shenmeng Xu, Lian Peng, Zhi Wang, Chuanli Wang, Chunbo Zhang, and Xianbing Wang, "Exploring Scientists' Working Timetable: Do Scientists often Work Overtime?" *Journal of Informetrics* 6, no. 4 (2012): 655–60.

15 Erin A. Cech and Mary Blair-Loy, "The Changing Career Trajectories of New Parents in STEM," *Proceedings of the National Academy of Sciences* 116, no. 10 (2019): 4182–87.

16 Interview 122 (female, sociology, Christian), conducted on May 14, 2019.

17 Ann Gibbons, "Key Issue: Two-Career Science Marriage," *Science* 255, no. 5050 (1992): 1380–82; Laurie McNeil and Marc Sher, "The Dual-Career Couple Problem," *Physics Today* 52, no. 7 (1999): 32–37; Hong Zhang, Julie A. Kmec, and Tori Byington, "Gendered Career Decisions in the Academy: Job Refusal and Job Departure Intentions among Academic Dual-Career Couples," *Review of Higher Education* 42, no. 4 (2019): 1723–54.

18 Interview 159 (female, physics, Christian), conducted on June 27, 2019.

19 As just some examples of research in this area, see: David Eggebeen and Jeffrey Dew, "The Role of Religion in Adolescence for Family Formation in Young Adulthood," *Journal of Marriage and Family*, 71, no. 1 (2009): 108–21; Christopher

G. Ellison, Amy M. Burdette, and Norval D. Glenn, "Praying for Mr. Right? Religion, Family Background, and Marital Expectations among College Women," *Journal of Family Issues*, 32, no. 7 (2011): 906–31; T. Frejka and C. F. Westoff, "Religion, Religiousness and Fertility in the US and in Europe," *European Journal of Population*, 24, no. 1 (2008): 5–31; J. E. Uecker, "Religion and Early Marriage in the United States: Evidence from the Add Health Study," *Journal for the Scientific Study of Religion*, 53, no. 2 (2014): 392–415.

20 Overall, 8 percent of the students reported having at least one child. This was slightly higher among male students (10%) and lower among female students (6%). A study found that in 2000, 13 percent of female graduate students had a child under five years of age, which steadily increased from the same percentage in 1990 (11.4%). It is not entirely clear whether the lower rate in my data are reflective of the narrower population (as that study examined all graduate students regardless of discipline or degree program), of actual declines over the past twenty years, or of some combination of the two. See Arielle Kuperberg, "Motherhood and Graduate Education: 1970–2000," *Population Research and Review* 28, no. 1 (2009): 473–504.

21 Among those with no children, the percentages saying that having children is very important are: 69 percent among very religious students, 47 percent among moderately religious students, 33 percent among slightly religious students, and 26 percent among nonreligious students.

22 For instance, an ordinary least squares regression analysis treating the religiosity predictor as categorical shows that the differences between the very religious group and the other three groups are not statistically significant at the $p<.05$ level, although two of the three are significant at the $p<.10$ level.

23 Lori-Turk Bicakci, Andrew Berger, and Clarisse Haxton, "The Nonacademic Careers of STEM PhD Holders," *American Institutes for Research*, April 2014, www.air.org; Arunodoy Sur, "Top 10 List of Alternative Careers for PhD Science Graduates," accessed December 31, 2022, www.cheekyscientist.com.

24 Diogo L. Pinheiro, Julia Melkers, and Sunni Newton, "Take Me Where I Want to Go: Institutional Prestige, Advisor Sponsorship, and Academic Career Placement Preferences," *PloS one* 12, no. 5 (2017): e0176977; Roberta Spalter-Roth, Olga V. Mayorova, Jean H. Shin, and Patricia White, "The Impact of Cross-Race Mentoring for 'Ideal' and 'Alternative' PhD Careers in Sociology," *American Sociological Association*, August 2011, www.asanet.org.

25 Janet D. Stemwedel, "Careers (Not Just Jobs) for Ph.D.s Outside the Academy," *Scientific American*, November 30, 2013, blogs.scientificamerican.com; Gina Shereda, "Academic Means More than Tenure Track," *Inside Higher Ed*, April 13, 2020, www.insidehighered.com.

26 John Robert Warren, "How Much Do You Have to Publish to Get a Job in a Top Sociology Department? Or to Get Tenure? Trends over a Generation," *Sociological Science* 6, no. 1 (2019): 172–96.

27 Interview 113 (female, psychology, pagan), conducted on April 30, 2019.

28 Interview 163 (male, chemistry, atheist), conducted on June 28, 2019.

29 Mary Ann Mason, Marc Goulden, and Karie Frasch, "Why Graduate Students Reject the Fast Track," *Academe* 95, no. 1 (2009): 11–16.

30 For a more technical analysis of the connections between religion, family and career goals, and intent to pursue different career options, see Christopher P. Scheitle, Brittany M. Kowalski, Erin B. Hudnall, and Ellory Dabbs, "Religion, Family, and Career among Graduate Students in the Sciences," *Journal for the Scientific Study of Religion* 60, no. 1 (2021): 131–46.

31 Scott Jaschik, "Rejecting the Academic Fast Track," *Inside Higher Ed*, January 15, 2009, www.insidehighered.com. Although research finds that teaching-focused institutions in academia are *perceived* to be more family friendly, it is worth acknowledging that this may not always be the case and might not even be the case on average. While research expectations tend to be much lower in teaching-focused institutions, professors in such colleges are usually have much heavier teaching loads, often have fewer resources, and are expected to provide high-quality mentoring for large numbers of undergraduate students.

32 Interview 150 (male, chemistry, Christian), conducted on June 13, 2019.

33 The sociologist Lisa Keister has examined how religious beliefs, practices, and identities influence stratification in the United States in general. Her work has also highlighted religiously influenced family formation factors as a key mechanism of such stratification. See Lisa Keister, "Religion and Wealth: The Role of Religious Affiliation and Participation in Early Adult Asset Accumulation," *Social Forces* 82, no. 1 (2003): 175–207; Keister, "Conservative Protestants and Wealth: How Religion Perpetuates Asset Poverty," *American Journal of Sociology* 113, no. 5 (2008): 1237–71.

34 A peer reviewer of a paper presenting some of the research in this chapter raised this question, asking, "If grad students in the sciences have values that lead them to 'focus on the family,' I can't help but wonder, 'So what?' Is there an inequity that is being exposed here?"

35 Wendy M. Williams and Stephen J. Ceci, "When Scientists Choose Motherhood," *American Scientist* 100, no. 2 (2012): 138–45. In my own survey data, I find that women are significantly more likely to say that having a satisfying marriage and having children is important to them. For instance, 40 percent of women in my survey say that having children is "very important" to them, as compared to 34 percent of men. Similarly, 75 percent of women say that having a satisfying marriage is very important to them, as compared to 70 percent of men. The design-based F-tests for both of these cross-tabulations are statistically significant at the $p<.05$ level.

36 Many of the family-friendly policies and programs implemented in US universities, including at my current institution, have been spearheaded by grants from the National Science Foundation's ADVANCE program, which for twenty years has

distributed over $270 million "to increase the representation and advancement of women in academic science and engineering careers." See National Science Foundation, "ADVANCE at a glance," accessed December 31, 2022, www.nsf.gov.

CONCLUSION

1 "Is Science Only for the Rich?" *Nature* 537 (2016): 466–70.
2 Sarah Benish, "Meeting STEM Workforce Demands by Diversifying STEM," *Journal of Science Policy & Governance* 13, no. 1 (2018): 1–6.
3 Kenneth Gibbs Jr., "Diversity in STEM: What it is and Why it Matters," blog post on *Voices* at *Scientific American*, September 10, 2014, https://blogs.scientificameri can.com. Emphasis in original.
4 The National Science Foundation, for instance, issues reports on the state of diversity in science focus on three groups: "Women, persons with disabilities, and some minority groups—Blacks or African Americans, Hispanics or Latinos, and American Indians or Alaska Natives." National Center for Science and Engineering Statistics, *Women, Minorities, and Persons with Disabilities in Science and Engineering: 2021*, Special Report NSF 21–321 (Alexandria, VA: National Science Foundation, 2021), https://ncses.nsf.gov.
5 Marcy H. Towns, "Where Are the Women of Color? Data on African American, Hispanic, and Native American Faculty in STEM," *Journal of College Science Teaching* 39, no. 4 (2010): 8–9.
6 Paul L. Hill, Rose A. Shaw, Jan R. Taylor, and Brittan L. Hallar, "Advancing Diversity in STEM," *Innovative Higher Education* 36, no. 1 (2011): 19–27; Erin A. Cech and Michelle V. Pham, "Queer in STEM Organizations: Workplace Disadvantages for LGBT Employees in STEM Related Federal Agencies," *Social Sciences* 6, no. 1 (2017): 12; Kumar Yelamarthi and P. Ruby Mawasha, "A Pre-Engineering Program for the Under-Represented, Low-Income and/or First Generation College Students to Pursue Higher Education," *Journal of STEM Education* 9, no. 3 (2008): 5–15.
7 Kent John Chabotar, "Valuing Diversity of Ideas," *Inside Higher Ed*, July 5, 2012, www.insidehighered.com; Alan Jacobs, "Creating Conservative Universities Is Not the Answer," *The Atlantic*, March 23, 2019, www.theatlantic.com.
8 Eric L. Goldstein, *The Price of Whiteness: Jews, Race, and American Identity* (Princeton: Princeton University Press, 2006); Rebecca Y. Kim, "Religion and Ethnicity: Theoretical Connections," *Religions* 2, no. 3 (2001): 312–29.
9 Khyati Joshi, "The Racialization of Hinduism, Islam, and Sikhism in the United States," *Equity & Excellence in Education* 39, no. 3 (2006): 211–26; Neil Gotanda, "The Racialization of Islam in American Law," *ANNALS of the American Academy of Political and Social Science* 637, no. 1 (2011): 184–95; Warren S. Goldstein, "The Racialization of the Jewish Question: The Pseudo-Secularization of Christian Anti-Judaism into Racial Anti-Semitism," *Religion and Theology* 27, no. 3–4 (2020): 179–201.

10 Alan S. Miller and Rodney Stark, "Gender and Religiousness: Can Socialization Explanations Be Saved?" *American Journal of Sociology* 107, no. 6 (2002): 1399–1423; Jessica L. Collett and Omar Lizardo, "A Power-Control Theory of Gender and Religiosity," *Journal for the Scientific Study of Religion* 48, no. 2 (2009): 213–31; Landon Schnabel, "More Religious, Less Dogmatic: Toward a General Framework for Gender Differences in Religion," *Social Science Research* 75 (2018): 58–72.

11 Devah Pager, "The Use of Field Experiments for Studies of Employment Discrimination: Contributions, Critiques, and Directions for the Future," *Annals of the American Academy of Political and Social Science* 609, no. 1 (2007): 104–33; S. Michael Gaddis, "Discrimination in the Credential Society: An Audit Study of Race and College Selectivity in the Labor Market," *Social Forces* 93, no. 4 (2015): 1451–79.

12 Although, it has been observed that outreach to some racial groups is sometimes similarly dismissed because it is assumed that those groups are already too skeptical of the science. See, for example, April Demboskey, "Stop Blaming Tuskegee, Critics Say. It's Not an 'Excuse' for Current Medical Racism," *National Public Radio*, March 23, 2021, www.npr.org.

13 Interview 135 (female, psychology, Christian), conducted on May 30, 2019.

APPENDIX

1 Elaine Howard Ecklund, *Science vs. Religion: What Scientists Really Think* (New York: Oxford University Press, 2010); Elaine Howard Ecklund and Christopher P. Scheitle. *Religion vs. Science: What Religious People Really Think* (Oxford University Press, 2017); Elaine Howard Ecklund, David R. Johnson, Brandon Vaidyanathan, Kirstin R. W. Matthews, Steven W. Lewis, Robert A. Thomson Jr., and Di Di, *Secularity and Science: What Scientists around the World Really Think about Religion* (New York: Oxford University Press, 2019).

2 Martin M. Chemers, Eileen L. Zurbriggen, Moin Syed, Barbara K. Goza, and Steve Bearman, "The Role of Efficacy and Identity in Science Career Commitment among Underrepresented Minority Students," *Journal of Social Issues* 67, no. 3 (2011): 469–91; Rachael D. Robnett, Martin M. Chemers, and Eileen L. Zurbriggen, "Longitudinal Associations among Undergraduates' Research Experience, Self-Efficacy, and Identity," *Journal of Research in Science Teaching* 52, no. 6 (2015): 847–67.

3 B. W. Roberts and R. W. Robins, "Broad Dispositions, Broad Aspirations: The Intersection of Personality Traits and Major Life Goals," *Personality and Social Psychology Bulletin* 26 (2000), 1284–96; Joan M. Barth, Sarah Dunlap, and Kelsey Chappetta, "The Influence of Romantic Partners on Women in STEM Majors," *Sex Roles* 75, no. 3 (2016): 110–25.

4 American Chemical Society, *ACS Graduate Student Survey*, 2013, www.acs.org.

5 D. R. Williams, Y. Yu, J. S. Jackson, and N. B. Anderson, "Racial Differences in Physical and Mental Health: Socioeconomic Status, Stress, and Discrimination," *Journal of Health Psychology* 2, no. 3 (1997): 335–51.

6 Chemistry was the largest, with 1,852 students, followed by physics (1,439), biology (1,401), psychology (955) and sociology (819).

7 The first paragraph of the email was changed to: "You were recently invited to take part in an online academic survey designed by researchers at West Virginia University and supported by a grant from the National Science Foundation. The purpose of this study is to better understand the backgrounds, experiences, and perceptions of graduate students. *As a small token of our appreciation for completing our survey, you will have the option of receiving a $5 Amazon.com Gift Code.* To complete the survey simply click on the link below to access the questionnaire OR copy and paste / type it into your browser window." This email was sent on February 12, 2019.

8 Note: Some early publications from this project mistakenly reported this as 1,307 complete responses and seventy-two partial responses. American Association of Public Opinion Research, "Response Rates: An Overview," accessed April 15, 2019, www.aapor.org.

INDEX

Page numbers in *italics* indicate Tables.

science, religion and diversity in: antagonistic atheism and, 144; laboratory
and, 137–38, 145; outreach in religious
communities, 143–44; religion as
beneficial part of, 145–46; religious
diversity, 142–46; student religiosity
by gender or race, 139, *140*; theology
and, 140–41
science graduate students: belief in God,
33; childhood religious affiliations,
43; concealing religious identity, *80*;
disciplinary differences, *39*; identity and purpose, 108; on negative
attitudes of others toward religion,
77; religion-science relationship, *52*,
52–53; religiosity by race and gender,
139, *140*; religious affiliations, *30*; religious affiliations compared to faculty,
32; religious service attendance of, *34*;
self-defined childhood religiosity, *44*;
self-defined religiosity, *36*, *42*; stigma
and hostility, 69–70
Science vs. Religion (Ecklund), 185n28
scientific community: with hostility
toward religion, 3, 7; with rules and
sanctions, 10, 11; science PhD programs and, 13; with shared connections, 8
scientific identity, religious and, 9, 13
scientists: becoming, 12–13; Christian,
108–9; elite, 40, 42, 181n40; on existence of God, 60; with faith, 116–17;
physical, 25, 38; in popular culture, 24,
191n4; on religion-science relationship, 51–52; religiosity of, 24–27, 32, 38,
40–41, 179n16, 181n40, 185n28; social,
24, 118, 139; students and self-worth as,
112; Union of Concerned Scientists, 58
scientists, religious: with boundaries between science and religion, 10, 177n18;
with counter-stereotypical natures,
9–12, 177n24; persistent interest in,

24–27; with science and religion, 4–5,
181n40
scientists-in-training, religious lives of:
affiliations, beliefs and behaviors,
30–36; Christians, 19–21; disciplinary
differences, 37–40; focusing on one in
five or four in five, 45; "greater" versus
"lesser," 40–42; Hindus, 21–23; with
isolation, 45; religiosity and cultural
affiliation, 36–37; religiosity of, 27–30;
religiosity of scientists, 24–27, 185n28;
religious origins, 43–44
sexism, 71
sexuality, 57, 169, 184n9
Shriver, Donald W., Jr., 38
Sikhs, 163, 165, 187n13
Smith, Christian, 190n13
social identity, 6–9, 37, 176n10
social sciences, 5, 16, 38, 39, 113, 114
social scientists, 24, 118, 139
sociologists, 38, 39
sociology graduate students: advisors and
peers, 98–99; Christians, 111, 121–22;
disciplinary differences, 39; on family
and career, 121–22, 126; identity and
purpose, 111, 113, 115–16, 119; proportion
of original invited sample by discipline,
153; religion-science relationship, 63–
64; stigma and hostility, 80–81
sociology PhD programs, 121–22
spiritual identity, 22, 113
spirituality: family life and personal reli-
gious/spiritual history, 173–74; religion,
science and, 172–73; religion and, 163–66
Stark, Rodney, 28–29, 30, 40
stereotypes: about abilities or commitment, 92, 121; internalized doubts
and, 83–85; religious diversity and
avoiding, 142–43; about religious students, 80–81; scientists with counter-
stereotypical natures, 9–12, 177n24;
threat experiments, 84, 85

ABOUT THE AUTHOR

CHRISTOPHER P. SCHEITLE is Associate Professor of Sociology at West Virginia University. He has published over one hundred peer-reviewed articles and three previous books, including *Religion vs. Science: What Religious People Really Think* (with Elaine Howard Ecklund). His research has been supported by a variety of funders, including multiple awards from the National Science Foundation.

www.ingramcontent.com/pod-product-compliance
Lightning Source LLC
Chambersburg PA
CBHW021845090426
42811CB00033B/2145/J